Whitetail Addicts Manual

Proven Methods for Hunting Trophy Whitetails

T.R. Michels

Creative Publishing
international

Minneapolis, Minnesota

Dedication

To Jesus, my God, Lord and Savior, I can do nothing without Him; to my father, Dr. Roger Michels, who introduced me to hunting, taught me ethics, morals, Christianity and the respect of the outdoors and its animals; to my mother Pat who provided me with encouragement, prayer and my first computer; to my wife Diane and my children, Melissa, Dallas and Tawnya, who understand my need to learn and to teach, and who put up with my hectic lifestyle. I could not have accomplished this work without their understanding, patience and support. Thanks to all of you, and God bless you.

T.R. Michels began using a duck call at age five, and hunting at the age of 15. Since then he has become a professional guide and outfitter. He has guided for elk, mule deer, white-tailed deer, bear, turkey and goose. T.R. has been published in magazines such as NRA's *American Hunter* and *InSights,* the NWTF's *Turkey Call, Petersen's Bowhunting, Buckmasters, Bow and Arrow Hunting, North American Whitetail, Fur-Fish-Game, Rublines, Wildfowl, Waterfowl, Big River Outdoors, Midwest Outdoors, Dakota Outdoors, Dakota Country* and the MDHA's *Whitetales.* He is recognized as one of the top hunting seminar speakers in the country.

Acknowledgments

Special thanks to the following people who provided research and shared their knowledge with me: Dr. Jim Cooper, Dr. Larry Marchinton, Dr. John Ozoga, Dr. Karl Miller, Dr. Kent Kammermeyer, Dr. Ben Koerth, Dr. Grant Woods, Dr. James Earl Kennamer, Dr. Lovett Williams Jr., Dr. Valerius Geist. To outdoor writer Norman Strung, and his wife Sil, who encouraged me to keep writing.

Creative Publishing international

Copyright © 2007
Creative Publishing international, Inc.
400 First Avenue North
Suite 300
Minneapolis, MN 55401
1-800-328-3895
www.creativepub.com
All rights reserved

Printed in China

10 9 8 7 6 5 4 3 2

Library of Congress Cataloging-in-Publication Data

Michels, T. R.
  Whitetail addicts manual : proven methods for hunting trophy whitetails / T.R. Michels.
     p. cm.
Includes index.
  ISBN-13: 978-1-58923-344-7 (hard cover)
  ISBN-10: 1-58923-344-1 (hard cover)
  1. White-tailed deer hunting. I. Title.

SK301.M43 2007
799.2'7652--dc22   2007007255

President/CEO: Ken Fund
VP for Sales & Marketing: Peter Ackroyd
Publisher: Bryan Trandem
Acquisition Editor: Barbara Harold
Production Managers: Laura Hokkanen, Linda Halls
Development Editor: Sharon Boerbon Hanson
Creative Director: Michele Lanci-Altomare
Senior Design Manager: Brad Springer
Design Managers: Jon Simpson, Mary Rohl
Illustrations &Charts: Danielle Smith
Page Layout: Danielle Smith

Text © T.R. Michels
All photos © T.R. Michels except:
Contributing Photographers: Mark Emery, Gary Kramer, John D. LaMere, Mark Raycroft, Ken Thommes, US Department of Agriculture, US National Park Service, Wildlife Research Center, Wisconsin Department of Natural Resources

CONTENTS

Introduction

In this age of computers, fast food and fast service you need to step back from the hectic pace of life and become part of nature to be a successful hunter. Think of yourself as a predator—as your ancestors were—and recover your predatory instincts.

To become a better hunter you need to understand the animals you hunt: their daily, seasonal and mating habits; how they communicate; their requirements for forage, security and thermal cover; and how they will react under the current weather, solar and lunar conditions. This will help you be better equipped to locate the "high-use areas" of feeding, watering, breeding, resting/thermal/escape cover, and the travel routes used by the animals. You also need to be able to interpret the signs they leave behind. Then, if you know the area you hunt as thoroughly as the animals do, you will be familiar with the best places to find the animals on a regular basis, based on the current conditions. You can accomplish all this by scouting, observing, recording and patterning the animal's movements.

When you are scouting and hunting you need to avoid being detected by the animal by what I call the "3 Ss"—Sight, Scent and Sound. You don't want the animal to see you, smell you or hear you. You can use products and techniques to camouflage or conceal yourself and your movement, to eliminate or cover your scent, and to keep you from being heard by the animals.

By understanding how the animals communicate and knowing their habitat requirements and activity patterns, you can attract them with the "3 Ss" using decoys, scents and calls; by improving the habitat; and by being in the right place at the right time. The best way to get an animal to come to you is to be in a place it is familiar and comfortable with, and already going to.

These are the keys to my hunting system. If you use them and put lots of time and effort into your hunting, you will become a better outdoorsman and hunter.

White-Tailed Deer Biology & Behavior

The white-tailed deer *(Odocoileus virginianus)* is the most numerous and most hunted big game species, and the most researched game animal in North America. As a result, hunters know more about white-tailed deer than any other big game animal on the continent. White-tailed deer reach lengths of 4 to 7 feet (1.25 to 2 m) and heights of 3 to 4 feet (1 to 1.25 m); males weigh 100 to 400 pounds (45 to 180 kg) and females 75 to 250 pounds (33 to 112 kg); and they live 5 to 10 years. They breed from October through January, with a gestation period of 6 to 7 months, resulting in 1 to 4 fawns each year, usually born in May and June. Both sexes grunt, snort and blow; fawns bleat. Males generally carry antlers with one main beam, with 1 to more than 6 points on each beam. Tracks are 2 to 3 inches (5 to 7 cm) long with the slightly smaller hind hoof landing in or near the front hoof track when walking. Droppings are often clumped or segmented cylinders in the spring and summer, and pellets during the fall and winter. During the fall and rut, males rub trees and thrash brush with their antlers. They chew low-hanging branches over scrapes on the ground, then dominant males often urinate in the same scrape after pawing them with their front hooves. They use these signs as a means of expressing dominance and leaving a message for females in estrus.

There are 38 recognized subspecies of whitetails occurring in North America, Central America and South America, with 17 subspecies living in the United States. Five of these subspecies are limited populations on islands off the southeastern coastal regions. White-tailed deer inhabit all of the lower 48 states, with limited populations in Nevada, Utah and California. They also inhabit all of the Canadian Provinces except the Northwest Territories and the Yukon. They are found in all of Central America, with the exception of the Baja Peninsula, and in the northern areas of South America.

Many whitetails find resting/secure/thermal cover and forage in hardwood forests.

The largest whitetail buck ever recorded was shot in 1926 by Carl J. Lenander in Minnesota. It weighed 402 pounds (181 kg) field dressed, with an estimated live weight of 511 pounds (229 kg). Several deer with live weights estimated in excess of 400 pounds (180 kg) have come from Iowa, Georgia, Maine, Minnesota and Wisconsin.

Because whitetails are a prey species, their senses and body style have evolved to avoid predators. They sense danger through their sense of smell (which is about 1,000 times better than humans'), by their sight (they see movement better than humans, but they cannot detect color as well), and by their hearing (about equal to human's). Their body style allows them to escape predators by running away and their body color allows them to hide well in many different types of habitat.

Most deer species evolved from forest dwelling animals. White-tailed deer primarily inhabit mixed hardwood forests and openings, preferring the secluded wooded areas for security, daytime core areas and bedding sites. They prefer meadows, prairies and agricultural areas for food sources. However, they have adapted to coniferous (evergreen) areas in the southeast, north and west; to swamps in the southeast, south and north; to prairie regions in the south and west; to mountainous regions in the east and west; and to any suburban habitat and metropolitan areas.

Feeding Habits

All deer species belong to the suborder Ruminatia, which means they are ruminants—they eat their food and store it in one of their stomachs, regurgitate it later and chew their cud to continue digestion. The result is that they feed heavily for a couple of hours in both the morning and evening, then generally move to either nighttime or daytime bedding areas and lie down to chew their cud.

As a result of being primarily a forest-dwelling animal instead of a plains, meadow or other open area species, whitetails developed into a browsing animal. They primarily eat the leaves, new shoots, twigs and mast (nuts, fruits and berries) of trees and shrubs, and forbs (wild flowering herbs). However, they are also opportunistic feeders, and readily eat grasses, sedges, domestic plants and vegetables and new growth leaves, stems, and grains of agricultural crops. They take advantage of any forage that they can digest and often use several food sources daily. In the spring, summer and fall, deer eat the stems and newly developed leaves of deciduous (hardwood) trees and shrubs such as sumac, red osier, maple, ash, hazel, alder, aspen and willow. New growth on coniferous trees (evergreens), especially cedars, and the tops of any new fallen trees are favorite foods.

In the summer, deer often eat grasses, sedges, forbs, the leaves and mast of shrubs, and the leaves and seeds of agricultural crops. As summer turns to fall, many of these foods lose chlorophyll, which means they become less tasty. This causes the deer to browse in wooded or brushy areas.

Oak tree mast (acorns) is a preferred food source wherever it is found. There are two main types of oak trees: white and red. Deer generally prefer the sweeter tasting acorns of white oaks which are produced yearly (red oak acorns are biannual). White oaks generally drop their acorns first, as early as August in some areas. In dry years, north- and east-facing slopes often receive the most moisture and those trees often produce the best acorn crops. Oaks at the tops of ridges usually drop their acorns first.

Whitetails utilize agricultural food sources, like this pumpkin and corn field (left). Acorns, like those of this red oak tree (right), are preferred food sources when they are ripe.

Deer generally prefer freshly dropped acorns rather than older, insect-infested acorns, which are easily identified by a small hole in the shell. During the fall, deer feed heavily on acorns, because they provide much-needed protein and carbohydrate content needed to get the deer through the breeding season, and the fat reserves they need to get through the winter. Deer that eat 1½ pounds (0.6 kg) of acorns a day per 100 pounds (45 kg) of body weight can easily survive three months of winter.

Deer feed heavily on standing corn where it is available, especially when it ripens in late summer or early fall. When deer eat corn, they tear it from the stalk and eat most of the ear, whereas squirrels and raccoons may eat only the tips and usually leave the ear on the stalk. Deer often take an ear of corn with them as they leave the field. Numerous ears of corn found in wooded areas usually indicate a deer-bedding site. In areas where agricultural fields cover much of the landscape, deer often use standing crops the same way they use wooded areas. Not only do they eat in the cornfields, but they often bed in them during both the day and night.

T.R.'S KEYPOINTS

Does may move more than normal during the rut, but often restrict their movements to particular portions of their home range, which makes them easier for the bucks to locate. Does may be found near their core areas, in traditional staging areas and communal scrapes near food sources, and in travel corridors leading to food sources.

Forage with high carbohydrates is sought during the fall to put on fat and get deer through the winter. Nuts, seeds, fruits of domestic and wild plants, agricultural crops of grains, and clovers are excellent food sources. Deer activity is influenced by the availability of these foods and the distance to them.

Bucks traveling through several doe-use areas may arrive at food sources after dark. They may also leave food sources later than normal in the morning. They may be seen during daylight hours in the morning as they go back to their core areas.

Home Range, Core Area and Bedding Sites

A lot has been written and said about whitetail home ranges, core areas and bedding areas. Unfortunately, much of it is based on the knowledge of deer in a particular area, or in a particular type of habitat. Whitetails inhabit many different types of habitats, such as dense hardwood forests, mixed woodland and agricultural, prairie, southern swamp, northern tamarack bogs, open or dense coniferous forests, open agricultural, semi-open river bottoms, and various mountain types. Because of this wide range of habitats, the daily habits of whitetails, their home ranges, core areas, and use of bedding sites varies greatly.

Home Range

Depending on the type and quality of the habitat, whitetails older than 2 to 3 years often have traditional areas, referred to as their "annual home range" that they use each year. Non-migratory deer may spend both the summer and winter on the same home range. In contrast, migratory deer in the northern states or mountainous regions may have two or more widely separated seasonal home ranges. Dr. Larry Marchinton, Dr. Karl Miller and other researchers have found that the home ranges of whitetails are generally from two to four times longer than they are wide. Deer in open coniferous or agricultural habitat may have irregular or circular shaped home ranges.

The size of a home range is governed by the availability of cover and food sources. Home ranges in monocultures of pine or hardwood forests, prairie river bottoms and primarily agricultural fields are larger than those in mixed habitats of wood lots, agricultural fields and river bottoms. The home range is generally restricted in size by topography. Mountains, ridges, bluffs, rivers and ravines obviously limit deer movement. The lack of cover in open prairies or agricultural areas inhibits daytime deer movement, and therefore usage by the deer. Home ranges are often preferred deer habitat in valleys or river drainages and the surrounding hills and woods.

The size of the yearly home range of mature bucks like this one often depends on the quality and diversity of the habitat.

When habitat size is limited, the home ranges of several deer often overlap.

The type and amount of food and cover determine how many deer a habitat can hold. The number of deer in a habitat affects the size of the home range of the deer. Deer in prime mixed habitats with abundant food sources generally have smaller home ranges (from 60 to 1,000 acres/24 to 400 ha) than deer in open coniferous forests, where food sources are low and widely scattered (up to 20 square miles/50 square km).

Climate directly affects the length and the use of the home range. In mild midwestern or southern climates, whitetails may have home ranges no longer than 2 miles (3 km), and they often have traditional core areas. Deer in colder, northern open prairie or foothill habitat may have larger home ranges (up to 120+ miles/192 km) and are less likely to have traditional core areas.

The climate and the number of bucks and does in an area affect the size of the home ranges of the bucks, especially during the rut. Buck home ranges are generally larger than doe home ranges, often two or more times the size of local doe ranges. Bucks in mixed woodland/agricultural habitat in the Midwest may have home ranges of less than 1,000 acres (400 ha), to 5 or more square miles (12 sq km) in size. Buck home range use varies by the season. During the summer adult bucks may use only a small portion of their home range. During the rut, adult buck home ranges often expand to include portions of several nearby doe and other buck home ranges.

Dr. Harry Jacobson calculated that the average annual range of does, in the hardwood forests of Mississippi, was 1,820 acres (728 ha); bucks had average ranges of 3,773 acres (1509 ha), with the largest range at 5,500 acres (2200 ha). Dr. James Kroll found that bucks in Alberta may occupy a 3,000 acre (1200 ha) core area and travel circuits of 20 to 25 miles (32 to 40 km) during the rut.

In many areas even non-migratory white-tailed deer may use four different seasonal home ranges–one each for winter, spring, summer and fall. In general, one end of the seasonal home range consists of the core area and daytime bedding sites, often in a wooded area, where the deer spend most of the day. The other end consists of an open feeding area, where the deer spend much of the night, and where they have night bedding sites. Generally speaking the seasonal home range of a deer is oblong or doglegged in nature, from three to four times longer than it is wide. These seasonal home ranges may be several miles apart or they may overlap each other. During the rut,

Core areas of deer, especially those of older bucks, are often in forests with fairly dense ground cover, where it is difficult to approach the deer without making noise.

the home ranges of bucks may be from 2 to 5 times the size of doe ranges, but they often restrict their movements to a small core area during the winter, spring and summer.

Depending on the type of habitat, these seasonal home ranges may be as small as 20 to 40 acres (8 to 16 ha) for does, and 1½ to 2 square miles (3.75 to 5 square km) for bucks, in the mixed hardwood/agricultural areas of the East and Midwest. Because does with fawns need plenty of forage, they often select core areas based on the availability of food, security and comfort. This core area is defended against other does, causing the does to spread out into available habitat to avoid conflict with each other. Because bucks need security, they generally select core areas away from other bucks, which are often more secure than does' ranges.

In northern hardwood forest, open agricultural country or western plains, both buck and doe home ranges may cover several square miles/km. Thomas Baumeister found that in Idaho's Clearwater River drainage the deer (including bucks) have summer ranges as small as 190 acres (76 ha) in the drainage's upper range. But in October and November, the deer migrated an average of 24 miles (38 km) to their winter ranges. Deer in northern Michigan, Minnesota and Wisconsin may migrate more than 100 miles (160 km) between fall and winter seasonal home ranges.

Whitetails may move several miles in the spring and fall as a result of snow depths, flooding or lack of food. The availability of food and the type of cover needed by the deer during each season determine which part of the annual home range the deer will use. For instance, deer using a soybean field in August may move several miles (kilometers) away during the rut or the hunting season.

Core Area

Within the home range of the deer is the core area, where the deer spends much of its time during the day. In some cases, the core area of an individual deer may be the same area used for one or more seasonal home ranges, but the area and size of them may vary. The deer may use the northern area

Daytime deer beds are often near trees such as this evergreen tree that provide some visual cover or protection.

in the summer and the southern area in the winter. It may use wooded areas in the winter to stay warm and open areas in the summer to stay cool.

Because the core area is used during the day, it typically provides security to the deer by a location in heavy cover, in inaccessible areas, such as a swamp or a steep hillside, or in a remote location. Core areas in heavy cover or on the downwind side of hills or woods also provide protection from the elements. The core area often contains readily available food.

Bedding Sites

Deer normally use different bedding sites for day and night, and may use different sites on different days depending on the wind speed and direction, temperature and precipitation. Deer spend the majority of the day in secure core areas, usually in the woods, where they can bed and feed. At night they often bed in or near open areas where they can lie down near food sources as they move and feed. In open terrain, both daytime and nighttime bedding sites may be located on hillsides, or in the middle of fields or swamps, where the deer can sense danger approaching and where they have one or more escape routes.

Although deer generally sleep during the day and feed at night, they often bed down to rest, ruminate and sleep near nighttime food sources. Because the vision of many predators is limited at night, deer feel more secure in open areas at night than they do during the day. Therefore, they may bed in open areas, often out of the wind, during the night. Night beds can often be found in fields, at field edges and in nearby brushy and grassy areas.

Deer may have one or more preferred bedding sites in their daytime core areas. The use of a particular bedding site is dependent on security and is generally governed by the direction of the wind, the temperature and the amount of precipitation. On hot, windy days deer may bed on an open shelf, or in the shade of a tall tree, where they are cooled by the wind. On hot days with no wind deer may bed in shaded or in damp areas. On cool days with no wind, deer may bed in areas that are out of the wind but open to the sun, where they receive warmth from solar radiation. On cold, windy days deer often bed in dense cover, or in low-lying areas where they are protected from the wind. When there is precipitation they often bed in areas with overhead cover. They may use evergreen stands where available, because evergreens reduce wind speeds by up to 50 percent, which results in less body-heat loss. These areas also allow the deer to smell and hear more acutely than in areas with high winds.

Deer—especially bucks—often bed with their backs to the wind, on a bench or rise where possible, where they can smell and hear danger from behind them and see and hear danger below and in front of them. In hilly or mountainous terrain, thermal currents generally begin to fall late in the afternoon and rise in the late morning. When deer bed high during the day, rising thermal currents bring scents to them.

Nighttime deer beds can often be found in open areas, like this CRP field, because the deer don't feel the need for visual security at night.

When the deer move down to feed in the evening, the currents may be still rising, bringing scent to the deer as they walk downhill. When deer bed in low-lying areas at night, the thermal currents carry scents down to them. When they make their way to higher daytime bedding areas in the early morning, the currents may be still falling, bringing scent to the deer as they walk uphill.

Deer bedding sites, especially those of older bucks, tend to be either in open, remote locations that cannot be approached without the deer seeing, smelling or hearing danger. Or they may be on the downwind side of hillsides or benches in thick wooded areas where the deer can see and hear danger from downwind, and see and smell danger from upwind. During the fall in the Midwest, where the wind often blows from the northwest, I often find buck beds on southeast-facing benches in wooded areas of dense underbrush, such as plum, briar (prickly ash) and buckthorn thickets.

Because their need for comfort and security changes throughout the year, the times of day when whitetails leave their bedding sites may change from season to season. In forested areas deer may begin to leave their daytime bedding areas an hour or more before sunset, and arrive at open area food sources at dusk or shortly after. In open areas, or after the leaves have fallen, deer usually get up and begin to move a bit later, often within half an hour of sunset.

Social Structure

The deer herds in an area are usually made up of a doe and her female offspring, and their female offspring. As long as there is available habitat and low competition for home ranges, the young females usually remain in the area where they were born. With death from natural causes and hunting there are often available home ranges for the young deer to occupy. Individual deer may defend their home ranges, but any one group of deer does not defend the habitat. The deer in these areas do not move as a unit, nor does the action of one deer determine the actions of the other, therefore the herd does not act as a cohesive unit.

Both bucks and does may make excursions outside their home ranges, but they usually do so only to find a new home range, or during the rut. There is generally little interaction between individual non-migratory deer herds because of the physical constraints of the habitat, and because newcomers are unknown and rarely accepted. Bucks 1½ years old are generally driven off the home range by their mothers, usually before the rut. However, some young bucks may stay on their mother's home range until their second year, when they leave to find their own home range. These young bucks often end up on home ranges in less preferred habitat.

According to researcher Anthony Bubenik, most ungulates (hoofed animals) have five maturity classes. These can be defined as: kids, pre-teens, teens, prime age and seniors. Each of these classes can generally be separated into male and female groups. Wildlife researcher Brown used four social classes in reference to white-tailed deer defined as: immature, subdominant floaters, group core members and dominant floaters.

Researcher John Ozoga combines these terms into what more clearly defines the social hierarchy of male whitetails. These social classes are:

- Kids (1½ years old)

- Subdominant floaters (1½ to 2½ years old)

- Fraternal group members (2½ to 4½ years old that have not reached maximum body and antler size)

- Dominant floaters (alpha or dominant breeding bucks 5½ to 9½ years old)

- Seniors (bucks past their physical prime, often non-breeding 8½ years or older bucks)

A shed with several points and good mass often indicate that a mature buck has used the area during the previous fall or winter.

Ozoga further divides the fraternal group members into primary group members (3½ to 4½ years old) and secondary group members (1½ to 2½ years old).

Ungulates include animals that produce horns (such as cows) and antlers (such as deer), and those that don't (such as horses). The horns or antlers of individual species are generally larger on males than they are on females, causing the males to look different from females. This difference in appearance makes males more susceptible to injury and death due to predation and hunting pressure. Because of this, males that carry antlers learn how to avoid predators, usually at a young age.

Antlers are shed yearly by male animals, making it difficult to distinguish males from females during some parts of the year. The absence of antlers makes the males less conspicuous and, therefore, less susceptible to predation, giving them a better chance of survival throughout most of the year. However, because antlers are used as a means of expressing dominance, and are used to attract females during the rut, they are often present during the rut, making antlered males highly conspicuous and susceptible to predation and hunting.

Prime-age males often carry the largest antlers. Senior males, even though they are not breeding, may still carry large antlers, making them also susceptible to predation. Because their advanced age does not allow senior males to escape as easily as younger males, they are extremely vulnerable. Both prime-age and senior males must become "smart" to avoid predation and hunting. The older the animal, the less likely it will participate in the rut, and the more likely it will choose secluded home ranges, travel at night, and limit its movements to avoid predation and hunting pressure.

In the case of the heavily hunted white-tailed deer, which is prized for large antlers, the males either learn to avoid hunters, or they are shot at and may die. Each year that a buck survives teaches it more about when and how to avoid hunters. Because of this, older whitetail bucks are smarter and warier than younger bucks. These infrequently seen, older trophy-quality bucks usually belong to the dominant floater or senior class.

While dominant floater bucks generally participate in the rut, they learn to move at times and in places where they are unlikely to be seen by hunters. Senior bucks (which may produce extremely large or heavy antlers), on the other hand, do not participate in the rut and may remain in secluded areas or become primarily nocturnal in their movements. Some younger bucks may not participate in the rut due to low social class, low testosterone levels, or other factors. Wildlife researcher Dr. Valerius Geist reports observing a buck that did not participate in the rut after it was beaten in battle by an older buck. Researcher John Ozoga observed a non-breeding buck that showed unusually high levels of the female progesterone hormone. During my own studies from 1993 to 1996, there were fewer sightings of subdominant bucks while the dominant bucks were engaged in rutting activity. A twelve-point buck that I observed for five years did not participate in breeding activity and was rarely seen during the last year of the study. This leads me to believe that any buck that does not participate in the rut is less likely to be seen during fall hunting seasons.

It is safe to assume that the older the buck is, the better it becomes at avoiding predation, hunting pressure and contact with humans. Because predation and hunting affect deer health and security, they can be considered as predatory behavior factors. Deer are subjected to predatory behavior throughout the year; however, they are subjected to hunting pressure primarily in the fall. Because of its seasonal nature, I refer to hunting and its associated activities that affect fall deer movement, as the hunting pressure factor. Both of these factors may cause a decrease in buck sightings during the fall. (There are other factors that can cause an increase in buck sightings during the fall, which I will describe in the following chapters.)

Daily Activity

Deer have evolved to avoid predatory animals during daylight hours. They are most active at sunset and sunrise, which scientists refer to as being crepuscular. Deer usually leave their secure daytime core areas about an hour before sunset

Young bucks (like this one in velvet) usually belong to the 2½- to 4½-year-old class known as "fraternal group members."

and move toward feeding areas. Before entering the first feeding area in the evening they may stop in a secure area often referred to as a staging area, where they may check the area with eyes, ears and noses. Once they feel secure they go into the feeding area. They often visit one or more feeding areas within the first few hours after sunset. After they are done feeding they often bed down in or near the feeding areas to chew their cud. This usually occurs within two to three hours after sunset. While they are in the nighttime feeding areas, they may get up and move about to urinate and defecate at about midnight, and then feed for a few minutes before lying down again, often in the same general area. In the morning they get up about an hour or two before sunrise to feed again before they move back into secure areas where they may lie down for a few hours before they go back to their daytime core areas, where they spend the day. They may get up periodically during the day to stretch, urinate, defecate and feed before lying down again.

When and where deer move on a daily and hourly basis is primarily governed by their needs, which include security, comfort, and forage factors. During the breeding season, deer are also affected by breeding behavior factors.

Security Factors

Because deer are a prey species their security depends on how well they avoid predators. Deer eyesight is better adapted to detect activity than human eyesight (but they don't detect color as well as humans). Their sense of smell is about 1,000 times better than that of humans, and their hearing is similar to that of humans. Deer generally feel secure in areas where they don't see, smell or hear anything that is unnatural or resembles predatory behavior, especially the sights, scents and sounds related to human behavior. When deer are active during the day they often travel at times when humans or predators are least active, or in areas where they don't detect human, predator-related or unnatural sights, scents and sounds.

A number of factors affect the security of the deer. Weather conditions such as the amount of cloud cover, precipitation, and the foliage on the vegetation determine how much light is available from the sun and moon, and how far the deer can see. Predatory behavior, such as the normal hunting activities of animals like wolves, coyotes, dogs, mountain lions and bears varies by area. Human intrusion, such as camping, nature walks, farming, scouting and hunting disrupt deer routines. Any and all of these factors can cause deer to become less active than normal during daylight hours.

How well a deer can see is dependent on three primary factors: the available amount of light; the amount and type of vegetation; and the openness of the terrain. Light and vegetation affect how well the deer can see; vegetation and terrain affect how far they can see.

Several different studies show that, during the fall rutting season, deer are affected by the available amount of light, whether it is sunlight or moonlight. During the day cloud cover, fog, snow and rain can all reduce the available amount of sunlight, which often results in deer moving more during daylight hours than normal, because the darker conditions make the deer feel secure. Depending on how cloudy, foggy or snowy it was during my study, the deer were sighted up to 20 minutes earlier in the evening and 20 minutes later in the morning on cloudy days than they were on clear days. During their study Mickey Hellickson, Larry Marchinton and Charles DeYoung found that bucks responded best to antler rattling when cloud cover was estimated at 75 percent.

Vegetation and Security

Vegetation affects both how far the deer can see, and the available amount of light. Thick vegetation, especially at ground level, reduces how far deer can see. During daylight hours, the thicker the vegetation is at ground level, the more secure the deer feel. The amount of foliage on the vegetation, especially overhead, affects how much light reaches the ground. During daylight hours, the more overhead vegetation there is, the less light reaches the ground, and the more secure the deer feel.

The amount of mutilation of the overhanging branch at this scrape indicates it has been moderately used, possibly by one or more bucks.

The amount of foliage on the overhead vegetation, and thus the amount of light that reaches the ground, changes in the autumn as the leaves fall. I first realized this in 1994 when I was hunting a big ten-point buck. The buck had been traveling a rub route paralleling a county road in September and October as it went to a cornfield to feed. Then, in late October, after the leaves fell, the buck (and all the other deer) stopped using the rub route trail and began using another trail farther into the woods, and farther away from the county road. I couldn't understand why the deer began using the new trail until I got down from my stand, stood on the deer trail, and looked around.

While the leaves were still on the trees and bushes earlier in the year I could not see the county road and the cars passing by. After the leaves had fallen, I could easily see the road, the cars, and the golfers on the golf course on the other side of the road. Obviously, the deer felt uncomfortable when they were using the first trail. To avoid being in the open once the leaves fell, they moved farther into the woods where they couldn't see the road, the cars or the golfers.

There was one other consequence of falling leaves. When the leaves were on the trees, the deer usually came down the trail to the cornfield about half an hour before sunset. But once the leaves had fallen they rarely used that portion of the trail more than 10 to 15 minutes before sunset. I suspect that the falling leaves allowed more light to reach the forest floor in wooded areas, which caused the deer to stay in the security of their bedding areas from 15 to 20 minutes longer than they did when the leaves were still on the trees. This is especially important to remember when you have patterned a buck. If you have been seeing the buck at 6:30 p.m. while the leaves were still on the trees, and then the leaves fall, don't expect to see the buck until 6:45 to 7:00 p.m.

The type of terrain often determines when and where a deer travels. In fairly flat terrain deer are often most active at sunset, during the night, and at sunrise. During the day deer may be active in remote areas, such as on the side of hills facing away from human activity where they don't see, smell or hear anything that alarms them. They may also move in areas where they can't see very far, like valleys and gullies between hills, in river and streambeds and in ditches or canals. I've seen deer moving in the pasture behind our house at noon with cars going by on the highway 75 yards (68 m) away. I know the deer couldn't see or smell the cars, and they probably couldn't hear them very well, so they felt secure.

Wind and Security

Because deer rely on their senses of smell and hearing to detect danger, anything that reduces their ability to hear and smell affects when and where they are active. High wind speeds affect how well deer can hear, especially when the wind blows through vegetation and rattles the leaves, grass, weeds, cattails, corn and the limbs of shrubs and trees. High winds can also bounce off trees in wooded areas making it difficult for deer to determine which way any scent carried on the wind has come from. Both of these conditions make deer nervous. During shifting or gusty winds deer usually seek protected areas or nervously bed and move throughout the day.

During my studies the combined sightings of all ages and sexes of deer were highest between 0 and 10 mph (0 to 16 km/h), and were minimal when wind speeds exceeded 10 mph (16 km/h). However, the sightings of the dominant bucks peaked between 11 and 15 mph (17 and 24 km/h). The majority of these dominant buck sightings between 11 and 15 mph (17 and 24 km/h) occurred during the rut, when the bucks were either looking for or with does. When the wind speeds were above 10 mph (16 km/h) I often saw the deer in heavy cover, in low-lying areas, or on the downwind side of hills and woods, where the wind speeds were lower than in open areas.

T.R.'S KEYPOINTS

Security needs cause deer to use available cover, travel in low lying areas where visibility is limited, move during low light conditions, and avoid predatory behavior when possible. Security to a deer is not seeing, hearing or smelling predators.

During the fall, deer begin to travel more at night as leaves fall from the trees, vegetation decreases and there is less daylight. The deer feel insecure because they can see predators farther away. They may abandon summer trails and seek out heavier cover or low-lying and less visible travel routes where they feel more secure.

High winds in wooded areas make it difficult for deer to hear sounds or smell scents and determine the direction of the scent source. They often stay near bedding sites or move in protected areas during high winds.

Conditions that cause a reduction in the normal amount of light (clouds, fog, precipitation) may cause deer to move earlier in the evening and leave later in the morning than normal because they feel secure.

Prolonged extreme weather makes security less important, causing deer to move earlier in the evening and later in the morning because of the need to eat.

Comfort Factors

Several different meteorological conditions affect the comfort of deer. Temperature, wind speed and direction, thermal currents, wind-chill, humidity, dewpoint, heat index and type and amount of precipitation determine whether deer feel comfortable. Like humans, deer have temperature, dewpoint, heat index, wind-chill, wind speed and precipitation factors in which they prefer to move.

Deer feel temperature factors (temperature, humidity, dewpoint, heat index and wind-chill) essentially the same way humans do. When it's hot, deer have a hard time cooling off, which makes them uncomfortable. When it's hot and

Lower temperatures may cause deer to move more during the warmer part of the day.

humid (creating a high dewpoint) they feel even more uncomfortable. When it's hot or the dewpoint is high, but there is a strong wind, the deer don't feel as uncomfortable, because the wind provides a cooling effect. When it's cold, deer lose body heat. Cold and damp together create a low dewpoint and they lose more body heat. When it's cold, damp and windy (creating low wind-chill factors) they lose even more body heat.

Temperature

Once the deer grow their winter coats in the fall, high temperatures keep them from traveling far during daylight hours. They usually wait until the sun goes down and the temperatures drop before moving to open areas to feed in the evening. When temperatures are low, deer often stay in areas providing protection from the wind. They move to areas open to the sun when there is no wind, or they wait until daytime temperatures rise, and move during the warmer part of the day, often in the late morning and late afternoon hours.

Relative temperature factors can cause heat stress in high temperatures and heat loss in low temperatures. In their study in Georgia, Drs. Kent Kammermeyer and Larry Marchinton found that lower temperature and dewpoint were "significantly correlated with greater deer movements in the fall." In other words, cooler temperatures in the fall resulted in increased deer activity after the deer had grown their winter coats.

M.E. Nelson found that deer in northern Minnesota regularly migrated when temperatures dropped below 19°F (-7°C) for five or more days. This suggests that when it gets too cold, the deer may migrate to warmer areas, or to areas where they can find relief from severe wind-chill factors and deep snow.

In the Great Lakes states deer often migrate to deer yards in coniferous forests. In mountainous regions, deer often migrate to semi-open or open areas at lower elevations.

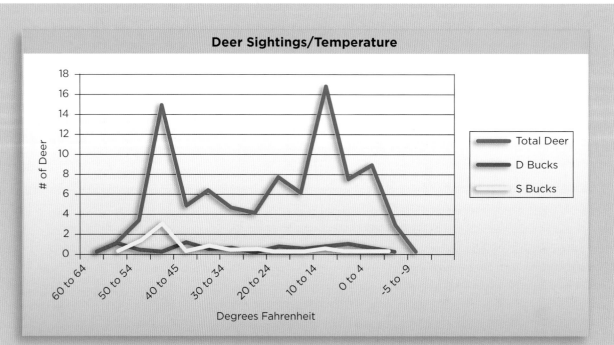

The above graph shows deer sightings from two different years in three different areas in southern Minnesota. There are five noticeable peaks in deer sightings. The highest peak occurred at 15°F (-10°C). Another peak occurred at 50°F (10°C) in the summer when the deer had summer coats. A medium peak occurred at 35°F (2°C), which often occurred in September. A medium peak occurred at -5°F (-20°C), often as the result of temperatures remaining below 0°F (C) for several days.

When the temperatures dropped below 15°F (-10°C) the deer moved even later in the morning than normal, but with fewer sightings, while evening sightings increased and occurred earlier in the afternoon than normal. The majority of the deer sightings below 5°F (-15°C) occurred in the afternoon, during the warmest part of the day.

Obviously deer in different areas react to temperature in different ways. During his studies in Texas John Stone found that the deer were active between 25 and 95°F (-4° and 35°C).

Dewpoint

The combination of humidity and temperature is referred to as dewpoint. During his study, Kent Kammermeyer found that deer activity was correlated with dewpoint. During my study deer were sighted most often when the dewpoint factors were between 5 and 55°F (-15° and 12° C), with most deer seen in the middle range (0 to 35°F/ -17 to 2°C). The sightings peaked at 25°F (-4°C).

After the deer grew their winter coats there were very few deer sightings when the dewpoint was above 45°F (7°C). There were also minor peaks in deer sightings at 55 and 5°F (12 and -15°C). The deer sightings at 55°F (12°C) occurred in September, before the deer had grown their winter coats. The sightings at 5°F (-15°C) often occurred after it had been cold for a period of days, when the deer were seen most often seen in the afternoon.

When the dewpoint fell below 0°F (-17°C) deer sightings were drastically reduced. I suspect that more deer sightings occurred when the dewpoint was between 5 and 40°F (-15° and 4°C) because the increase in humidity caused the dewpoint to feel warmer than the actual temperature. When the dewpoint was below 20°F (-6°C), the deer were seen later in the morning and earlier in the evening than normal, with most of the sightings in the evening. When the dewpoint dropped below 15°F (-9°C), twice as many deer were seen in the evening as in the morning. When the dewpoint dropped below 10°F (-12°C), five times more deer were seen in the evening than in the morning.

Since temperature factors often affect when and where deer move, those same temperature factors may affect how frequently bucks make or check rubs and scrapes.

During my deer research in Minnesota I found that, in the fall and winter, the majority of the deer sightings occurred when the temperature was between 0 and 65°F (-17 and 18°C), with most sightings between -10° and 50° F (-23 and 10°C), and they occurred between an hour before and an hour after both sunset and sunrise. Peak sightings occurred between 15 and 30°F (-9 and -1°C). When the temperatures fell below 20°F (-6°C), morning deer sightings occurred from sunrise to an hour and a half after sunrise, with very few sightings before sunrise; evening deer sightings occurred from an hour and a half before sunset until an hour after sunset, with several sightings after sunset.

Degrees	Activity	Result
10 to 19°F (-12 to -7°C)	Some late and early morning movement.	
20 to 49°F (-6 to 9°C)	Normal morning and evening movement.	
Over 50°F (10°C)	Restricts activity to darkness when temperatures are cooler.	Winter coats make heat uncomfortable for the deer; they may bed in areas open to the wind, but out of the sun, or in damp areas.

Daytime Temperature or Dewpoint (temperature and humidity combined). The flexible temperature parameters given here apply to whitetails in the northern half of the United States and Canada. I stress the word "flexible" because deer in different areas have different tolerances to different meteorological conditions. Data from Texas suggests that southern deer are more tolerant of high temperatures, and because they are not subjected to the extreme cold of the northern states and Canada, they are probably less tolerant of low temperatures. Individual deer even have different tolerances. Bucks will move in almost any weather condition in search of estrus does during the rut.

Wind Speed

Wind speed can affect the comfort of the deer by its cooling affect when temperatures are high, and by making it feel colder when temperatures are low. When it was hot I often sighted the deer on hills open to the wind, in shaded or wet areas, or under trees with few lower branches, where the deer could lay in the shade and be cooled by the wind. When it was cold I often sighted the deer on the downwind side of hills and woods or in low-lying areas where the wind speed was lower.

During my studies deer sightings were fairly consistent in wind from 0 to 10 mph (0 to 16 km/h). But, once the wind speed reached 10 mph (16 km/h) deer sightings decreased, and as with cold temperatures, the deer were found in heavy cover, in low-lying areas, or on the downwind side of hills and wooded areas out of the wind. Deer sightings in open areas dropped significantly when the wind speeds exceeded 15 mph (24 km/h), and deer sightings in open areas were almost nonexistent when the wind speeds exceeded 20 mph (32 km/h).

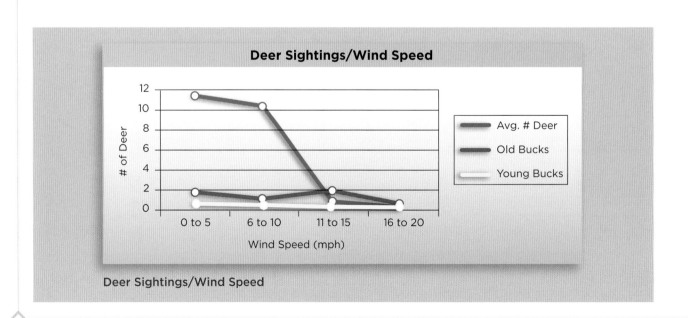

Deer Sightings/Wind Speed

Wind Speed	Deer Activity	Result
0 to 5 mph (0 to 8 km/h)	Best	
6 to 10 mph (9 to 16 km/h)	Some	
11 to 15 mph (17 to 24 km/h)	Limited	During high winds deer have a hard time hearing and smelling; they feed and bed on the downwind sides of hills and woods. Deer may use benches ¼ to ⅓ of the way down the hill, in the calm pocket where wind speeds are lower.
20+ mph (32 km/h)	Minimal	

Wind Speed

In relation to wind speed, the combined sightings of all the deer decreased at about 10 mph (16 km/h). But, as with temperature factors, the bucks reacted to the wind speeds differently than the does. During the rut younger buck sightings peaked at 5 mph (8 km/h) and then dropped off. Older trophy-class buck sightings peaked at 10 mph (16 km/h) and continued up to 20 mph (32 km/h).

Thermal currents affect when and where deer move because air currents affect both the comfort and the security of the deer. When the weather is hot deer may seek areas where there are cool thermal currents, and they avoid areas where there are thermal currents when it is cold. Thermal currents generally rise in the morning as the air temperature rises, and fall in the evening as the air temperature falls.

In hilly or mountainous regions deer often bed on benches on the downwind sides of hills during the day, about a third of the way down the hill, where the wind speed is not as high, and where they can detect scents on the rising currents. When the deer move downhill to feed in the late afternoon they are able to detect scent on the thermals that may still be rising. During the night deer often bed in low-lying areas, where they can detect scent on the falling currents. When the deer move uphill to bed during the morning, they are able to detect scent on the currents that may still be falling.

Wind-chill

The combination of wind speed and low temperature is referred to as the wind-chill factor. Deer sightings in relation to wind-chill factors showed even more dramatic results than sightings in relation to temperature or dewpoint. Most of the fall deer sightings occurred when the wind-chill factor was between 5 and 40°F (-15° to 4°C). There were very few deer sightings when the wind-chill factor was above 45°F (7°C). This

Direction	Time	Result
Rising	Morning	Sunlight causes air to warm and rise. In hills or mountains game will often bed uphill during the day to catch rising scent.
Falling	Evening	Darkness cools air causing downward currents. Game may bed low at night to catch falling scents. As animals move uphill in the morning they catch the scents on the still-falling thermals.

Thermal Currents

Degrees	Activity	Result
Below 0°F (-17°C)	Restricts movement.	
0° to 9°F (-17° to -12°C)	The combination of wind and low temperature decreases the temperature factor. Deer feed and bed on the downwind side of woods and hills.	May move late morning and early evening when temperatures are warmest.
10° to 19°F (-12° to -7°C)	Some movement.	
Above 20°F (-6°C)	Good movement.	When there are high temperatures or dew-points high wind speeds can create lower wind-chill factors, which may increase deer activity during normal activity times, especially if there is cloud cover.

Daytime Wind-chill

was to be expected because there were very few deer sightings when the temperature was above 45°F (7°C). However, light winds can actually increase deer movement when the temperature is high, because the winds provide a cooling effect. Peak deer sightings occurred when the wind-chill factors were between -5 and 25°F (-20 to -4°C).

Most doe activity occurred between 10 and 40°F (-12 to 4°C) wind-chill, and peaked at 15 and 35° (-10 to 2° C) wind-chill. Most of the younger buck activity occurred between 20 and 55° wind-chill (-6 to 12° C), and peaked at 25 to 45° (-4 to 7° C). Most of the older trophy class buck activity occurred between 5 to 40° (-15 to 4° C) wind-chill, and peaked at 15 to 35° (-10° to 2° C), which was almost exactly the same as the does. I suspect that the younger smaller-racked bucks moved at different times than the does and the older bucks in an effort to avoid the aggressive older bucks during the rut.

The graph on page 25 shows combined deer sightings from two different years in three different areas. The minor peak at -25°F (-31°C) was the result of consistently low temperatures in January and February, after many of the food sources had been depleted, when the deer were seen either early in the afternoon or late in the morning at remaining food sources.

Open area beds, like this one on a field edge, are often used primarily at night, especially when temperature is conducive to deer movement.

The sightings on the Watson and Eagan property paralleled each other because they were both in areas where the deer could be protected from the wind by hills and woods, when the deer were sighted in both the mornings and evenings. The sightings on the Houghlum property were fairly consistent because they were on the south side of an open hill, out of the prevailing winds, where the deer were seen primarily in the evening. However, they were seen bedded near the food source in the mornings when the temperatures were below 0°F (-17°C). It was obvious that they had spent the night there instead of returning to their normal daytime core areas.

Humidity and Precipitation

Cloud cover often keeps the temperature and humidity high, which makes deer feel uncomfortable. In my studies I found that when there was cloud cover and the temperatures were high, deer activity was often minimal, due to the high humidity and heat index factors.

Rain can cause deer to lose body heat. When it's cold, heavy precipitation causes the deer to lose body heat. Consequently they stay in secure bedding areas, or they seek areas that protect them from precipitation. However, when it's hot, deer may move when there is light to medium rain because it provides a cooling affect. In his study on deer activity Hofacker reported that deer hunters saw more deer when there was no precipitation. Researchers Progulske, Duerre, Tibbs, Hawkins, Klimstra and Michael all found that deer activity decreased during periods of rain.

Precipitation of any kind (rain, snow, drizzle, fog and mist) diminishes the available amount of light, which may cause the light conditions to resemble dawn and dusk. As a result of this, deer may move and feed during the day when there is light rain, drizzle or snow, because the low light factor and limited visibility make them feel secure. However, they don't often move during heavy precipitation, because they not only feel uncomfortable, they also can't see or smell very well. If heavy precipitation persists through one or more morning and evening feeding periods the deer may begin to feed shortly after the precipitation lets up, or after the temperature warms. During heavy precipitation, especially hail, deer seek cover in wooded areas or thick undergrowth.

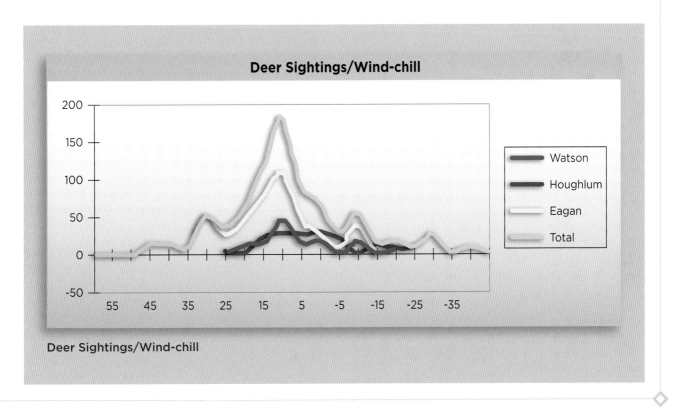

Deer Sightings/Wind-chill

Precipitation	Movement	Result
Fog, drizzle, light rain, light snow during the day	Good.	Light precipitation reduces the amount of light and makes deer feel secure.
Moderate to heavy rain	Some.	Precipitation is uncomfortable and may cause deer to lose heat.
Heavy rain, sleet or hail	Restricts.	Reduces the ability to see and hear, probable loss of body heat. Deer seek cover.
Medium to heavy snow	May increase.	Snow decreases the amount of light and visibility distances, which may make deer feel secure during the day, provided there is no wind. They may move.

Precipitation To Movement Comparison

During my studies the older bucks did not move much during medium to heavy rain. However, once the does came into estrus, they often moved during moderate to heavy precipitation, because the does remained in their core areas, which made them easy for the bucks to locate. Because snow can reduce the available amount of light and limit visibility I often saw bucks moving when it was snowing, as long as the wind speed was low. Many older bucks have also learned that few hunters are out during heavy rain or snow.

Barometric Pressure

During my seven-year study I found that approximately 40 percent of the deer sightings occurred when the barometer was rising, 40 percent occurred when the barometer was falling, and 20 percent occurred when the barometer was steady. I did find that more deer were seen when there were abrupt barometric changes than when the barometric pressure was steady. I found no evidence that deer began to feed prior to the arrival of a storm, suggesting that they knew or "felt" that a storm was approaching. However, deer were frequently seen feeding after storms let up, especially if the storm lasted a day or more.

In his study in Georgia, Kammermeyer found that deer activity was correlated with barometric pressure changes in the morning and evening. But, he noted that this is when these barometric pressure changes normally occur in that area.

Illinois biologist Keith Thomas found that the highest amount of white-tailed deer movement and feeding activity occurred when the barometric pressure was between 29.80 and 30.39. I suspect that deer may react to the weather changes associated with barometric pressure changes, such as wind speed, wind direction, temperature factor changes, cloud cover and precipitation, but not necessarily to minute changes in barometric pressure.

Winter coats are a measure of protection against severe elements.

Weather Findings

The results of my studies suggest that low wind-chill factors result in increased deer movement. However, when I looked at the time of day when the deer were sighted (in relation to sunrise and sunset), it became apparent that deer activity during normal daytime activity times actually decreased when the wind-chill factors were below 20°F (-6°C).

Instead of deer sightings occurring within the normal activity times of an hour before and an hour after sunrise and sunset, they occurred from as early as three hours before sunset to sunset, and from sunrise to three hours after sunrise. In other words, low wind-chill factors resulted in decreased deer sightings during normal daylight activity times, and increased deer sightings during the middle of the day, probably because the deer preferred to move during the warmer portions of the day.

There was also a minor peak in deer sightings when the wind-chill factor dropped to -5°F (-20°C). As with low temperature and low dewpoint these wind-chill deer sightings occurred earlier in the afternoon than normal. In another one of my studies there was a minor peak in deer sightings between -30 to -20°F (-34 to -28° C). However, these sightings were all in January and February, when it had been cold for several days. I suspect these extreme cold temperatures forced the deer to move in order to find food so they could create body heat and stay warm.

My findings on temperature, dewpoint and wind-chill indicate that cold, windy weather is more of a deterrent to deer activity than cold, damp weather, and that hot, humid weather is more of a deterrent than hot, windy weather. The findings also suggests that wind-chill (not temperature or dewpoint) is often the determining temperature-related influence on deer activity in the fall and winter, especially when the temperatures are low. I also suspect that the heat-index is often the determining temperature-related influence on deer activity in the spring and summer, especially when the temperatures are high.

Reaction to Hunting Pressure

I often hear whitetail hunters complain that they don't see as many bucks during the hunting season as they do during pre-season scouting, and that the trophy bucks they saw during their scouting sessions seem to disappear during the hunting season. Many hunters attribute this lack of buck sightings during the rut to the belief that bucks become "nocturnal," or because they leave their home ranges during the hunting season. Do some bucks pull a vanishing act during the hunting season?

Studies by several deer biologists show that deer, especially older bucks, react to hunting pressure in different ways. During their study to determine whether the deer became nocturnal or left the hunting area when the season was in progress, Missouri researchers caught several deer in traps. One of the bucks was caught in the same trap a month after it had first been trapped. After that it was not seen for the next two years, until it was shot 200 yards (180 m) from the original trapping location. In spite of being pressured by hunters, one other deer stayed in the same 40-acre (16 ha) area during the entire hunting season. The researchers felt that these deer had not left the hunting area, but had avoided the hunters by becoming less active, moving less, and by moving mostly after dark.

In another Missouri study researchers found that bucks moved about 5 miles (8 km) a day during the pre-hunting season. Then, when the firearm season began the bucks reduced their activity by 20 percent, traveling only about 4 miles (6.5 km) per day. The bucks that had home ranges partially inside a refuge shifted most of their activity to the refuge while the hunting season began. The only time they reportedly left the refuge was at night.

Bucks may also relocate to avoid hunters. During a study on the DeSoto National Wildlife Refuge several deer left the area when the hunting season opened. They swam across the Missouri River into Iowa. When the Iowa hunting season opened they swam back to Missouri. During the muzzleloader season eight deer moved into a strip of posted "no hunting" land 60 yards wide by 100 yards long (55 m by 91 m), and stayed there until the season was over.

During their study on the effects of human disturbance on whitetail bucks Mickey Hellickson, Scott Rhodes, Larry Marchinton and Charles DeYoung found that when bucks from 1½ to 11½ years old were approached from downwind they moved from 1,511 to 2,120 feet (453 to 636 m). They found that 3½ to 4½-year-old bucks traveled the longest distances, and 7½-year-old and older bucks traveled the shortest distances. In general, they found that the older the buck was, the shorter the distance it traveled after it had been disturbed. This suggests that older trophy class bucks often learn to avoid hunters by moving less, relying on hiding techniques rather moving.

Whitetail Communication

Deer species, including white-tailed deer, communicate through sight, scent and sound. A wide variety of body postures and movements are used to communicate by sight. Their sense of smell is very well developed, so they have a number of scents and scent organs to communicate by smell. They also communicate through sound by vocalization, blowing through the nostrils and thrashing branches.

Young bucks may become "movers" during the rut, resulting in fewer buck sighting at that time.

BUCK AND DOE ACTIVITY DIFFERENCES

Like many whitetail hunters, I am primarily interested in when and where the bigger bucks are most active, particularly the older, trophy-class bucks. So, I broke my deer sightings down into doe and fawn sightings, and young and old sightings. During the study I found that bucks often traveled in different areas and at different times than does. I also found that bucks often moved during different weather conditions than does, and that older trophy-class bucks moved during different weather conditions than the younger smaller-racked bucks.

Because bucks are more susceptible to predation and hunting, they are more security conscious than does; the older a buck gets, the more security conscious it becomes. Throughout the study the bucks moved later in the evening and earlier in the morning than the does, and they usually traveled in more secure areas and denser cover than the does did during daylight hours.

During the pre-rut and scraping phase, the trophy-class bucks left their bedding areas about 20 to 30 minutes after the does in the evening, and they began moving back toward their bedding areas about 20 to 30 minutes earlier than the does in the morning. However, this changed during the pre-primary scraping and primary breeding phases (the peak of the rut), as the dominant bucks began to travel at approximately the same time as the does. Once most of the older does were bred the bucks again began to leave their bedding areas later than the does in the evening, and they began moving toward their bedding areas earlier in the morning than the does. This occurred during the rest phase.

Body Language

Whitetails use several different movements and body postures when they interact with other deer, and as they react to the different sights, scents and sounds around them. Their body language may be used to warn of danger, to threaten a predator, or engage in dominant behavior with other deer, such as the following.

Foot Stomping: Deer often stamp their front feet when alarmed to alert other deer of danger. The foot stomp may also be used to try to startle a predator. The excess interdigital scent left on the ground during the foot stomp may also tell other deer that a deer felt endangered in the area where the scent was left.

Tail Flagging: Deer use a tail-waving motion as they flee, probably to warn other deer of danger, and to show other deer which way the flagger is going. Does flag more often than bucks; a running deer that is not flagging may be a buck.

Head Bobbing: A deer sensing danger may lower its head as if to feed, and jerk its head back up again quickly. The head bob may be an attempt to catch a predator moving while it thinks the deer is feeding. The quick head bob may also be used to startle a waiting predator into giving its position away. The head bob may be used after a foot stomp.

Tail Flicking: A deer will remain still as long as it does not flick its tail from side to side. Once the tail starts to flick the deer may be getting ready to move.

Ear Twitching: A doe with its ears forward or relaxed is usually alone or with its fawns. A doe twitching its ears to the side or backward is probably listening to her fawns or other deer. A doe turning its ears or head to the rear during the rut may have a buck following it.

Hoof Pawing: Deer paw to dig up food under snow and heavy vegetation, to dig up minerals, and to clear away sticks, stones and snow before lying down. Bucks may paw and sniff the ground when making a scrape under an overhanging branch. When a buck paws slowly while making a scrape it may stay awhile, if it paws, stops, looks around, and paws again, it may be getting ready to leave.

The tail-waving of this doe (left) is an alarm signal to all other deer in the area. Neither of these deer (right) appears to be in an aggressive, threatened or alarmed posture, because their ears are relaxed.

Both bucks and does exhibit aggressive body behavior in various situations to communicate, such as the following.

Walk Toward: The aggressive deer walks toward another deer. This is the lowest level of aggression.

Ear Drop: The deer lays its ears back along its neck with the ear openings facing out. This is low intensity aggression that is frequently used.

Head High Threat: The deer stands erect, holds its head high, tilts its nose upward, and lays its ears back. The tail of the deer may be held half way out. This is a rarely used threat.

Head Low Threat: The deer lowers its head and extends its neck toward another deer, with its ears laid back. This is called the "Hard Look" by deer biologists.

Head Raise: The head of the deer is pointed in the direction of another deer, the head is snapped up and backward, and then back to a resting position.

Lunge: The deer lunges with its head toward another deer without making contact.

Front Leg Kick: A dominant deer strikes at a subdominant with a forefoot one or more times. The hoof does not necessarily hit the other deer. Also called the Strike.

Charge: The deer runs rapidly at another deer, but stops before contact is made.

Chase: A subordinate that does not respond to a lower level of aggression may be chased by a dominant, while the dominant uses the head low posture as it pursues the subdominant.

Rake: A dominant lifts a foreleg about 18 inches (45 cm) above the ground and drags it across the back of a subordinate. It is used by a dominant to displace a subordinate from a bed.

Poke: One deer contacts another with its nose. This is commonly used to direct group movement or to displace another deer.

Head Shake: The deer lowers its head, and spreads its forelegs to lower the front of the body, while it shakes its head from side to side with its ears flopping. A high intensity threat usually performed at a distance.

Body Push: The aggressive deer approaches another deer and pushes against the rear of the other with its shoulder while laying its throat on the back of the other deer.

Sidle: Two deer walk slowly side by side in a head high threat posture. Bucks usually turn their head and body slightly away from each other in a show of redirected aggression. If neither deer retreats, one or both of the deer may flail at the other with their forefeet or rush the other deer.

Rear Up: A deer rears up on its hind legs. This is usually preceded by a head high threat.

Flail: Deer stand on their rear legs and strike out with both forefeet at each other. Flailing continues until one deer quits. This is the most intense form of aggressive behavior exhibited by does, and by bucks without antlers.

The following aggressive body behaviors are used exclusively by bucks.

Nose Licking: The buck licks its nose constantly from both sides of its mouth.

Crouch: The buck lowers its head and tilts its antlers toward an opponent. The aggressive buck is usually hunched, with all four legs partially flexed, lowering its height.

Dominance Walk: During the breeding season high-ranking bucks' hair often stands on end and it may walk slowly with a stiff-legged gait.

Circling: The aggressive buck slowly circles its opponent while crouching.

Antler Threat: A buck lowers its head so that its antlers point directly at another buck. If the other deer uses an antler threat, a rush usually follows.

Antler Thrust: A buck rapidly lowers its head pointing its antlers toward the side or rump of another deer and then abruptly raises its head. Bucks may do this to both bucks and does. It does not always result in contact.

Sparring: Two bucks lock antlers and push and twist their heads back and forth. This is a non-violent contest between bucks of all sizes. Unfortunately, the bucks may remain together afterward, sometimes leading to death of one or both deer.

These two bucks with evenly matched antlers are only participating in a sparring match, not a full-blown fight.

Rush: The rush is a rare form of aggression usually between two aggressive, large bucks. Both bucks lunge at each other with an antler clash. They may attempt to push or pull each other backward or sideways. Their hair often stands on end and the white hairs of the metatarsal gland are often visible. Bucks frequently grunt and snort during a rush.

Scent Glands and Organs

Deer use scents pheromones and hormones to communicate their sex, sexual readiness, dominance, their travel route and direction, and alarm. They can track and recognize other deer by scent. They either leave scent on themselves (self-impregnation) or they leave scent on the ground and vegetation, and at rubs and scrapes. These scents are so specific that deer can distinguish individual scent no matter how many other deer are in the area.

Here is a list of the glands that produce many of these deer scents.

Forehead Glands: The forehead or sudoriferous glands are located between the top of the eyes and the antlers. The scent from these glands is used for recognition and to establish dominance. Prior to the rut, bucks take part in social grooming, sniffing and licking each other's forehead and tarsal area. During the rut, when sparring and fighting begin, dominance is established. Bucks then recognize each other by scent and associate it with social level. The activity of these glands has been positively correlated with age and probable social status. The glands are most active in older, dominant bucks producing an oily substance that makes the hair appear dark. The oil is transferred to rubbed trees and the overhanging branch at scrapes when the head of the buck comes in contact with the tree, and is used by dominant bucks to advertise their presence to both sexes. Marking trees and branches with forehead scent is a way to display dominance and foster recognition among bucks. Dominant bucks create the most rubs and they rub more often than subdominants. The scent from the forehead glands may be used as a priming pheromone, when left in areas used by does, to bring does into estrus and to synchronize the timing of the rut between bucks and does.

Pre-orbital Gland: Located at the inside corner of the eye, this gland is controlled by muscles. It may be opened by rutting bucks to signal aggressive behavior. Females open this gland when tending fawns. The opinion that secretions from this gland are rubbed on overhanging branches, may not be correct.

Nasal Gland: These two almond-shaped glands are located inside the nostrils and are probably used to lubricate the nose. They may also be used to leave scent on overhanging branches.

Vomeronasal Organ: This diamond-shaped organ located on the roof of the mouth serves some of the same purposes as the nose. It is used primarily to analyze urine (possibly while performing the lip curl and sniff), or Flehmen gesture, when a buck curls its upper lip and sucks air into its mouth so that scents come in contact with the vomeronasal organ. It is usually performed by a buck that is with or trailing an estrus doe. Analysis of urine through the vomeronasal organ may help to synchronize the breeding readiness between bucks and does, and ensure that both sexes are in peak breeding condition at the same time.

Salivary Glands: These glands inside the mouth produce saliva that contains enzymes to help in digestion. The enzymes in the saliva may contribute to the scent left on the overhanging branch at scrapes, and on rubbed trees when a deer licks or chews a branch or a tree.

Interdigital Glands: These glands are located between the toenails of all four hooves of white-tailed deer. The scent is left each time the deer takes a step. It is also left in large amounts when a deer stomps its hoof, and when a buck makes a scrape. Some of the compounds in the scent of mature males (3½+ years) may be present in higher concentrations, which alerts other deer of the presence of a dominant buck. Additionally, does use this scent to track their fawns, and bucks use it to track does. Because scent molecules evaporate at different rates deer can determine which way another deer went by the amount of interdigital scent left behind. The scent from these glands is the primary tracking scent.

Preputial Gland: This gland is located on the inside of the buck's penal sheath and may be used for lubrication.

Metatarsal Glands: These glands are a light tan circle of hair of about 1⅔ inches (4 cm) in length located on the outside of the hind leg between the toe and the hock (or heel) on whitetails. They are not actual glands, because they have no duct. It is not totally understood in whitetails, but I have seen it flared when two bucks fight. White-tailed deer exhibit the smallest glands. The black-tailed deer are larger, and mule deer have the largest. It has been suggested that blacktails open this gland when alarmed to express danger.

Tarsal Glands: These true glands appear as a tuft of erectile hairs, measure about 4 inches (10 cm) in diameter, located on the inside of the hind leg near the hock. The scent from this gland is the primary recognition scent of deer. The lactones of these glands are specific and allow other deer

This buck is performing "Flehmen gesture," which allows it to sample the estrus state of the urine, by use of the vomeronasal organ on the roof of its mouth.

to determine the age and sex of the deer leaving the scent. The strong smell of the tarsal gland is caused by the deposit of urine on the deer's gland during rub-urination. Rub-urination occurs when the deer brings the back legs together and urinates over these glands. All deer rub-urinate, often just after rising from their beds. Bucks rub-urinate to display social dominance and they determine social ranking by sniffing each other's tarsal. Bucks rub-urinate more frequently during the rut while making scrapes. Does rub-urinate to make it easier for their young to follow them, and possibly to express social status among doe groups. Young animals rub-urinate to self-mark. Part of the function of the scent from this gland may be to act as a warning signal. Deer often sniff and lick each other's tarsal area during social grooming for identification, which reinforces the social hierarchy.

Urine: Bucks smell estrogen in the urine of sexually ready-to-breed females. It has been suggested that does smell testosterone and protein levels in buck urine and are able to determine the health of the buck by the smell. This allows them to choose a healthy, dominant buck to breed with. The combination of scents left behind by a buck during rub-urination at a scrape (urine, testosterone and tarsal) may serve as priming pheromones to bring does into estrus.

Many bucks form bachelor groups and travel together prior to the rut. They often groom each other's head/neck region, and know each other's smell by the forehead, tarsal, metatarsal and interdigital scents. Older bucks exert dominance over subdominants throughout the year by threats such as kicking with the foreleg and attacking with the antlers. When sparring begins in the fall, the younger bucks already know which other bucks are dominant and stronger. They also know which dominant used a rub, overhanging branch and scrape by the smell left behind. This eliminates much fighting.

Vocalizations

Through research we know that deer use different sounds to express alarm and distress (Alarm/Distress), to express dominance/threaten other

deer (Agonistic), to keep in contact with each other (Social Contact) and to solicit attention from and respond to does and fawns (Maternal/Neonatal). Deer also make sounds associated with courtship and breeding behavior (Mating). The statistics on whitetail vocalizations shown in the chart are based on studies by Dr. Larry Marchinton. The duration of the calls is approximate. The tone of the call usually depends on the deer. Larger deer, especially bucks, tend to make deeper sounds.

The snort and the bawl are alarm or distress sounds. The snort is an intense blowing sound produced by expelling air through the nostrils. It's best described as a loud whew, or whew-whew-whew, but it may also sound like a whistle. It may be heard farther than ¼ mile (0.4 km). Deer that see or hear a disturbance but cannot smell the source often use repeated low snorts, foot stomping, head bobbing and tail flipping, possibly to alert other deer of danger. A deer's sense of smell is thought to be independent of conscious discrimination. Deer that smell danger usually snort, then flee while flagging the tail. The bawl is an intense call used by deer of all ages when they are in distress—caught by a predator, trapped or injured. The sound is a loud "baa." Does often respond to the call by running in, presumably out of maternal instinct.

The agonistic sounds, in the form of grunts, are used in three different forms to express dominance or to threaten another deer. Grunts are also used

When this fawn wants to be fed, or its mother calls to it, it will use a "fawn mew."

Type	Call	Duration (seconds)	Pitch	Tone	Volume
Alarm/Distress	Snort	.25	high	low or high	high
	Bawl	1.00	low-high-low	moderate	high
Agonistic	Low Grunt	.25	level	low	low
	Grunt-Snort	.50	low-high	low	moderate
	Grunt-Snort-Wheeze	2.50	low-high-low	high	low
Social Contact	Social Grunt	1.00	low-high-low-high-low	moderate	moderate
Maternal	Maternal Grunt	.25	rising	low	low
Neonatal	Fawn Mew	.50	low-high-low	low	low
	Fawn Bleat	.50	low-medium-low	low-medium	low-moderate
	Nursing Whine	.50	low-high-low	low	low
Mating	Tending Grunt	25 to 4 minutes	low	low	moderate
	Tending Click	10 to 1 minute	staccato	low	moderate
	Flehmen Sniff	50 to 1 minute	low	low	low

Vocalizations at a Glance

to locate other deer that then respond by either coming to the call or announcing their location by returning the call. The low grunt is used by both does and bucks throughout the year. It sounds like a soft guttural "err." This is the first level of aggression, used along with body language to displace lesser deer. If the lesser animal does not move, it is usually rushed and may be kicked with a forefoot by the dominant. The grunt-snort is the second level of aggression and is made by adding one or more snorts to a grunt sounding like an "err-whew." The grunt-snort is used most often by bucks during the breeding season in more intense situations. The grunt-snort-wheeze is the most intense form of an aggressive call. It consists of a grunt-snort followed by a drawn-out wheeze through pinched nostrils. The wheeze may sound like a whistle.

The social contact grunt is often performed by members of a doe group when they become separated. It may help deer stay in contact when they can't see each other. In one study, only females performed this call. This call is longer than the low grunt. It can be heard by humans from as far away as 109 yards (100 m). It may attract bucks during the breeding season.

Does and fawns interact with a number of maternal or neonatal sounds. The maternal grunt is a low, quick grunt performed at short intervals as a doe approaches a fawn's bedding site. The fawn generally leaves its bed and joins the doe. This sound is audible to humans only a few yards (meters) away. It is similar to a low grunt but often louder. It may be heard up to 100 yards (91 m) away. The mew is used by the fawn when it wants attention, or is given in response to the maternal grunt. The bleat is the fawn version of the bawl. The fawn bleats when it wants urgent attention, is hungry, or wants care. A bleat may be heard from as far away as 109 yards (100 m) by humans. The nursing whine occurs while the fawn nurses or searches for a nipple.

Bucks use specific mating sounds during the rut. The tending grunt is a low grunt used by bucks when pursuing an estrus doe. It may be a single short grunt, several grunts or a long drawn-out grunt. It is probably given to alert other deer of the presence of a dominant in order to keep them away and to attract does. The tending click is a clicking sound bucks may make when looking for or following estrus does. It sounds like someone slowly running a fingernail across the teeth of a comb. It appears to be a slow, drawn-out version of the tending grunt. The bellow is a long, very intense call that seems to be a louder and longer version of a tending grunt. The Flehmen sniff is a low sound produced during the lip curl (when air is inhaled to bring urine/pheromones in contact with the nose or vomeronasal organ), allowing the buck to determine the breeding readiness of a doe.

Although several call manufacturers, writers and speakers claim there is an estrus doe bleat or doe mating call, no call of this nature was noted in the scientific studies I have read (that doesn't mean a doe doesn't use a call when it is in estrus). This sound may actually be the social contact grunt, or a variation of it, used when the does are in estrus.

The Rut

Most deer hunters know that whitetails act differently during the rut than they do at any other time of the year. After spending time with, and talking to, a number of different whitetail hunters, most of them experienced and some of them quite knowledgeable, I realized many did not understand the progression of the rut, or the time frame of the rut. Most of them knew that in the upper Midwest, rubbing usually begins in September, scraping in mid October, and that the peak of the rut occurs during the middle of November. But there seemed to be a difference of opinion about what the peak of the rut meant. To some it meant the time when they most often saw bucks during the day, usually the two weeks before the breeding phase. Others thought the peak of the rut meant the peak breeding activity time, which it does. Some who thought all the breeding activity occurred during the week of the peak of the rut resigned themselves to the

belief that once the peak of the rut was over, no more breeding would occur and if they did not get a buck by the peak of the rut there was no reason to hunt as hard, because there would be less activity.

Rubbing, scraping and breeding all have their own time frames (which overlap each other), and their own peaks during the rut. Rut related activity in northern areas usually starts when bucks begin making scrapes and rubbing small trees and brush to remove velvet from their antlers. This may occur as early as late August or early September in areas above the 38th parallel. Rubbing may peak in mid September and generally diminishes throughout the rut, but it may rise again during later breeding phases. Scraping activity may begin as early as the first week of September, but without much activity until mid to late October. Breeding may begin in mid October, and breeding begins to increase as scraping increases in late October. Scraping often peaks from mid to late October as bucks continue to make new scrapes and maintain existing scrapes. As breeding activity increases in early November, scraping activity decreases. Breeding in northern areas may be intermittent from mid to late October, fairly continuous throughout November, with peak breeding occurring sometime between the first and the third week of November, and intermittent from early December into January. What was that about breeding beginning in mid October?

The graph on page 63 shows the breeding dates of over 1,600 does in Minnesota between 1980 and 1987. It clearly shows that that breeding of both yearling and older does begins in mid October and continues to mid January, for a breeding season length of 120 plus days. It shows that peak breeding during all years, and for all years combined, occurs during the second week of November. In addition, it shows that rarely do any more than 25 to 30 percent of the does in any one area get bred during the one-week time frame of the peak of the rut. It also shows that doe fawns in Minnesota breed from late October to early February, and that peak breeding of doe fawns occurs from late November to late December.

Chronology of the Rut

There are several problems with trying to explain the timing of the activities of the rut. While the three main activities of the rut (rubbing, scraping and breeding) have their own time frame, one activity does not stop when another starts—all three activities overlap each other and often occur at the same time. Another complication is that each buck may go through its own set of activities, independent of the other bucks in the area. Older, dominant bucks in the over-4½-year-old class usually begin shedding velvet, rubbing and scraping earlier than 2½- to 3½-year-olds. And while 1½-year-old bucks do rub, they may not scrape or breed at all, depending on the buck-to-doe ratio and the age structure of the bucks in the herd.

One of the purposes of my seven-year study on whitetail behavior was to determine when the different activities of the rut occurred, and how they interacted. These activities include rubbing, scraping and breeding. When the weekly number of each of these activities is placed on a graph they each exhibit their own curve. The peak of the breeding curve is defined by most researchers as the peak of the rut.

In their Georgia study of rubs and scrapes Terry Kile and Larry Marchinton classified rubs into three types on the basis of exposed xylem (light-colored wood beneath the bark). Because little

of the bark was removed, Type 1 and Type 2 rubs were not as visible as Type 3 rubs. Type 1 rubs included all trees with broken trunks, which were most common during the first two weeks of September. These rubs decreased rapidly and became negligible by the end of October. Type 2 rubs included trees that were lightly damaged with little or no exposed xylem, which also peaked early and then decreased. High visibility Type 3 rubs were in the minority in September but increased steadily until all rubbing ceased. In another Georgia study Larry Marchinton, Karen Johansen and Karl Miller found that dominant bucks rubbed most in September prior to breeding, while subdominants rubbed most in October and November. Rubbing by high-ranking bucks may help establish dominance, mark areas where they are dominant prior to breeding, and physiologically prepare does for the rut. Bucks of all social ranks marked overhanging branches and inspected those that had been marked by other bucks.

In many areas of North America dominant bucks begin rubbing in late August and early September to remove velvet. Most early rubbing occurs on saplings about 1 inch (2.5 cm) in diameter in or near buck bedding and core areas. Most of these early rubs will be Type 1 that are broken, and Type 2 with little bark removed. Peak rubbing usually occurs from mid to late September. By mid October dominant bucks begin traveling outside

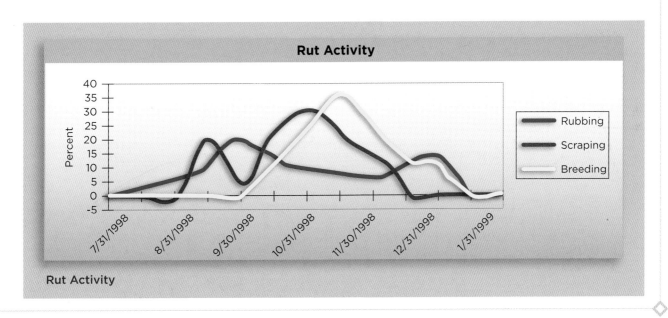

Rut Activity

While these bucks may "check" scrapes all year long, they won't usually rub their antlers on the overhanging branch at the scrape or chew it, until they shed the velvet from their antlers.

their core areas, making visible Type 3 rubs along rub routes that they, or other bucks, have used in past years. They also make rubs in staging areas near nighttime food sources used by both bucks and does. In the Midwest, I start seeing rubs along breeding range rub routes in mid October. Rubbing activity generally diminishes after the bucks begin scraping, but may continue as long as there are does are in estrus, as late as mid December in northern states.

In the above-mentioned study Marchinton, Johansen and Miller divided scrape activity into three separate acts:

- overhead branch marking, in which the buck mouthed a low hanging branch and rubbed the forehead, mouth, nose and chin on the branch, while frequently pausing to sniff and chew/lick the branch.

- pawing the soil, possibly leaving interdigital scent on the ground.

- rub-urinating, in which the buck placed its rear legs close together and urinated on its tarsal glands.

The researchers found that overhead branch marking (regardless of pawing) continued sporadically from January through March, increased in April and May, decreased in June, increased again in July and often peaked in August. The researchers also found that dominant bucks marked branches more often than subdominants in May and again in August.

Pawing scrapes under overhead branches began in June, with a marked increase in activity in August and September. Pawing peaked in October, and diminished through November and December. Pawing by high-ranking bucks peaked in October, just prior to peak breeding, and was much more frequent than pawing by subdominants throughout the rut. Pawing of subdominants peaked in October and November, which may explain the increase in scrape activity just after peak breeding.

There is some evidence that, depending on the age structure of the herd, older dominant bucks will mark overhead branches, paw and rub-urinate at a scrape; that 2½- to 3½-year-old bucks will mark the overhead branch and paw, but not rub-urinate; and that 1½-year-old bucks will mark the overhead branch but not paw or rub-urinate.

Scraping in the fall in the upper Midwest starts shortly after rubbing begins in September, but may be sporadic until after rubbing peaks in late September/early October. The first scrapes I see occur during early September along rub routes near doe core areas, and at the edges of open meadows and food sources. These scrapes may be used every two to three days and then be abandoned for two to three weeks before being used again in late October. These first scrapes often occur under licking branches that are used all year long.

Many hunters never see these early scrapes because they don't look for them. Even if they did, the scrapes are not very noticeable, they may not have any bare ground, and only have small amounts of grass pushed toward the back of the scrape. My studies show that scrape activity often ceases when nighttime temperatures rise above 45°F (7°C) in the north. This may be the cause for intermittent scraping in September and early October.

As the nights get colder in mid October, scrape activity increases again and usually peaks in late October/early November, just before breeding activity peaks. My studies indicate that from 1994 to 1998 most scraping activity in late October/early November occurred at scrapes that had been used earlier that year. Many of these were traditional scrapes (they had been used for three or more years) that were either in doe core areas or near nighttime food sources.

Once the does come into estrus, scraping activity diminishes as the bucks search for and breed does. During my scrape studies I saw very few reused or newly made scrapes between November 7 and 21. When scraping activity did occur it was again at scrapes that had been used earlier that year, and had been used in previous years. Very few of the scrapes that first appeared after November 18 (after peak breeding) were ever used again. On November 21, 1996, I watched a dominant buck make five scrapes around my tree stand in half an hour–they were never used again. I suspect that these "one-time" scrapes are made by dominants simply out of rutting urge, and by

subdominants that begin scraping because the older bucks are too busy with does to threaten or chase the younger bucks.

Estrus Cycles

My own observations, those of several other writers and photographers, and the studies of Dr. Larry Marchinton in Georgia show that breeding occurs as early as September 24 in northern Minnesota, October 15 in southern Minnesota, October 17 in Georgia, and October 24 in central Wisconsin. Thanks to Marchinton's studies we can pinpoint estrus cycles in captive deer. The study was conducted to find out how many estrus cycles unbred does would experience. During the study recurrent estrus ranged from 2 to 7 times. Of the eight does studied one 2½-year-old came into a first estrus on October 17, another 2½-year-old on October 24, three 1½-year-olds on November 11, one 2½-year-old on November 19, one 1½-year-old on November 21, and one 5½-year-old on December 1. The last recurrent estrus occurred on April 7.

This shows that, even without recurrent estrus, some does will be in estrus from mid October to early December, resulting in a breeding period of more than 45 days. In northern areas the breeding period may last in excess of 60 days, from mid October to late December. In southern areas it may last more than 90 days, into February. In most areas a small portion of the adult does may be bred in October, most of them in November, and a few more in December. This is typical of most deer populations. In northern areas 1½-year-old does may experience their first estrus in December. Doe fawns (5+ months) may experience their first estrus and breed in December, January or February.

During his Georgia research, Marchinton found that the estrus cycles of does are quite variable. Instead of occurring every 28 days as previously thought, the estrus cycles of the does in the study ranged from 21 to 30 days, with an average of 26 days. This makes it difficult to pinpoint the timing of the late breeding phase, especially when coupled with the knowledge that the first estrus of a doe may occur from mid October to the first part of

December. Marchinton also noted that the does were in estrus from 24 to over 48 hours, not the 24 hours previously thought. Any buck chasing a doe may spend up to three days with her without returning to its core area.

My studies in Minnesota show that roughly 10 to 20 percent of the does come into estrus during the early breeding phase, 50 to 60 percent during the 2 to 3 weeks of the primary breeding phase, and 20 to 30 percent during the late breeding phase. It made no difference if I considered the estrus dates of the does from October through December, or only the estrus dates in November, the peak of the rut occurred within seven days of November 10. The primary breeding phase usually lasted three weeks, from approximately November 1 to 21.

Breeding

Most deer biologists believe it is the decreasing number of hours of daylight during the fall (referred to as photoperiod) that triggers the rut in white-tailed deer. In northern regions above the 40th parallel whitetails generally breed when there are 9½ to 10 hours of light per day. This photoperiodic change occurs once every year, roughly every 365 days, and so does the rut. But, the rut for deer herds in different areas may vary by days or weeks.

As does come into estrus, bucks become more focused in the search to find them.

The breeding phase for deer in each area is primarily triggered by the number of hours of sunlight each day or the photoperiod. Since whitetails inhabit a large portion of North America and Central America, the geographic location of individual deer herds determines when breeding should occur. The rut is governed by the timing of spring. In order for fawns to survive they need weather warm enough that they won't die of exposure, and weather that is wet and sunny enough to produce new forage, so the does can produce milk for the fawns. Deer in the north have short breeding periods because they have a late spring and early fall, resulting in short summers. Deer in the south do not have to breed as early, and have longer breeding periods because of the long summers and late fall. Whitetails in the southern United States may have up to a five-month breeding period (September to January). Deer above the 40th parallel generally breed when there are approximately 10 hours of sunlight per day, which occurs in early November.

Through selective survival over several generations, deer have adapted so that they breed approximately 200 days before the arrival of spring in their area. To ensure that at least some of the fawns survive each year, not all of the does breed, or produce fawns, at the same time. An extended fawning season ensures that some fawns will live even when there is a late spring. Because of this, the length of the breeding season in most deer herds lasts six or more weeks, which makes it hard to predict when peak breeding will occur.

Robert McDowell completed an interesting study titled "Photoperiodism Among Breeding Eastern White-tailed Deer" in 1970. This study documented the breeding dates of whitetails from the 28th parallel to the 48th parallel. The dates given cover a broad range as the study covers the entire eastern half of the United States, from approximately the Rocky Mountain foothills east. Obviously, the breeding dates in each area will vary based on local weather conditions and the genetics of the herd.

Several factors besides latitude and photoperiod may cause fluctuations in the rut. When local deer populations are not balanced properly

Parallel	Breeding Dates	Peak Breeding
Below the 28th	First week of August through the last week of February	First week of September through the second week of October, from the third week of November through the first week of December, and from the second week of January through the first week of February
Between the 28th and 32nd	Second week of September through the first week of February	Peak breeding from the first week of November through the first week for February
Between the 32nd and 36th	First week of October through the first week of January	Peak breeding from the first to the fourth weeks of November
Between the 36th and 40th	Second week of October through the last week of January	Peak breeding from the first to the third week of November
Between the 40th and 44th	First week of October through the last week of January	Peak breeding from the last week of October to the second week of November
Between the 44th and 48th	Last week of September through the last week of November	Peak breeding from the first week of November through the first week of December

Robert McDowell Photoperiodism Study

(many are not), the timing of the rut may be affected. If there are not enough mature bucks to leave priming pheromones at rubs and scrapes for the does to come in contact with, some of the does will not come into estrus, or be bred, during the normal breeding period, causing them to breed later than normal. The amount of forage in the habitat and the health of the deer also affect the timing of the rut. Undernourished and unhealthy does may come into a first estrus later than other does.

Genetics can play a large part in when deer breed, as shown from a study in Louisiana. In 1983 researchers found that deer in the Camp Avondale Boy Scout Reservation in East Feliciana Parish bred from November 6 to 26, with a median date of November 12, a full month earlier than the deer for the rest of the parish. The reason for this earlier breeding is because the deer in the camp were relocated from a herd in the Red Dirt Management Game Management Unit, where breeding occurs earlier.

Doe activity changes during rut. During the breeding phase, researchers Ozoga and Verme found that does move shorter distances per day than usual and concentrate their activities on a small portion of their range. They concluded that during peak rut, does walk a lot in small areas in an effort to attract bucks. This behavior ceased after the rut. They found that does become about 28 times more active than normal one to two nights before they came into estrus. However, most of their daytime activity (when they could legally be hunted) was restricted to the hours between 5 and 8 a.m. This suggests that the best time to look for bucks that are looking for does would be the early morning hours.

The researchers concluded that the does' increased activity in a small area, prior to and during the time they are in estrus, makes it easier for the bucks to locate the does. It might also explain why bucks tend to cluster their scrapes in particular areas (such as doe core areas and staging areas near nighttime food sources). The researchers also concluded that if a doe is not located by a buck by the time she is in estrus, she might begin to wander in an effort to find a buck, or have it find her.

In areas where there are older dominant bucks, yearling bucks make about half as many rubs as older bucks. When there are few older bucks, younger bucks may rub more. Abundant rubs may indicate several dominants, or few dominants.

Rubbing begins as much as two months before the primary breeding phase, and usually peaks about a month before the peak breeding. The decline in rubbing often coincides with a rise in scraping activity.

The first rubs (Type 1) to appear are usually on small saplings, often leaving the tree broken but with little bark removal. These rubs decrease early in the rut and are replaced by rubs with minor bark removal (Type 2). These rubs are usually replaced by rubs with much of the bark removed (Type 3), that are often on large trees.

When buck territories overlap, bucks often paw the ground, and thrash brush and small trees with their antlers. Torn-up areas indicate places frequented by more than one buck.

Low acorn production may cause a decrease in rubbing and scraping, because bucks spend more time in search of food. Less scent-marking activity during some years may not mean fewer bucks, but less forage.

Peak scraping usually signals the beginning of breeding. Usually a small percentage of does are bred in October. Peak breeding in northern areas (above the 38th parallel) normally occurs during the second week of November. A late breeding phase of fawns (not one-year-olds as previously thought) may occur about a month after the older does have been bred.

Rut Phases

As a result of my studies I recognized eight different rut phases with their associated activities. The phases are pre-rut, dispersal, pre-breeding, primary breeding, post primary breeding, rest, pre-second breeding, and second breeding, all followed by the post rut. It is often difficult to distinguish when these phases start and end, because their activities overlap, and because dominant and subdominant bucks are on different time schedules.

The following are the rut phases with approximate dates for northern areas.

Pre-Rut/Rubbing Phase (Rubbing/Scraping) Sept. 1 to 25: During the pre-rut, when bucks are beginning to rub to shed velvet, most of their activity will be in or near their core areas that contain bedding sites and late summer food sources of mast, berries, succulent grasses, clovers and agricultural crops. Scraping often begins at this time, especially if nighttime temperatures fall below 45° (7°C). Dominant bucks create most of these early scrapes. My studies show that bucks travel primarily at dawn and dusk during this phase.

Fall Home Range Shift/Dispersal Phase (Rubbing/Scraping) Sept. 15 to Oct. 15: Bucks with rising testosterone levels become more aggressive and no longer travel in groups. Bucks in some areas may shift from a summer core area to a fall core area, and begin to use larger home ranges as they search for preferred food sources to put on fat for the winter. They may travel through several doe home ranges in preparation for breeding. Scraping may diminish at this time. My studies show that bucks begin to leave core areas later in the evening, and go back to core areas earlier in the morning during this phase.

Pre-Primary Breeding/Peak Scraping Phase (Rubbing/Scraping/Chasing/Breeding) Oct. 15 to Nov. 5: Two to three weeks before the primary breeding phase, bucks begin to travel their rub routes, making rubs and scrapes. Most of the scrapes at this time are still made by dominant bucks. While most scent-marking activity occurs at night, bucks do travel their rub routes in cover during the day making rubs and scrapes. During the evening, bucks generally follow a rub route from a core area, through doe-use areas, to night time food sources, then trail back through doe use areas to buck core areas in the morning. Scrape activity usually peaks at the end of this phase. My studies show that bucks may travel to food sources in the early afternoon and search for does until late in the morning. During the full moon I often see bucks along their rub routes an hour or more before sunset. Some does may come into estrus and be bred during this phase. Because bucks are exerting dominance, they are extremely aggressive and will fight almost anything. Does that are not ready to breed at this time often run from bucks, hence the term "chasing phase."

Primary Breeding Phase (Rubbing/Scraping/Breeding) Nov. 1 to 25: Once the does come into estrus the bucks will travel during all hours of the day in search of them. The bucks may stop traveling their rub routes, and follow doe trails instead. Rubbing and scraping by dominants usually diminishes at this time because the bucks are searching for and breeding does. However, subdominant bucks may create fresh rubs and scrapes because the dominant bucks are more interested in does than making rubs and scrapes or exerting dominance over the subdominants. Although the full moon may not cause increased activity during peak breeding, daytime buck activity will be high as long as does remain in estrus. Generally there is above normal daytime deer activity during the two to three weeks when the does are in estrus, no matter what the moon phase is. However, if the buck-to-doe ratio is low you may not see many bucks during this phase, because the bucks may all be with does. Some hunters refer to the lack of buck sightings at this time as "The Buck Lockup."

Post-Primary Breeding Phase (Searching/Scraping/Breeding) Nov. 20 to 25: After most of the does have been bred some dominant and subdominant bucks may travel their rub routes, and visit doe-use areas and food sources during the day, especially if there is a full moon. My studies show that bucks may move at any time of the day during this rut phase, no matter what the moon phase is.

Rest Phase Nov. Nov. 20 to Dec. 5: During the two to three weeks after the post-primary breeding phase bucks that took part in breeding may stay in their core areas, where they feed on mast, any remaining green grass, leaves or clover, and agricultural crops or browse. Most buck activity will occur at night or in secure wooded areas during the late evening and early morning hours. The full moon may cause bucks to become active during the day, but I seldom see dominant bucks outside their core areas during this phase. Rubs and scrapes occurring outside buck core areas at this time may be made by subdominants.

Pre-Late Breeding Phase (Rubbing/Scraping/Searching/Breeding) Dec. 1 to 10: Two to three weeks after peak breeding some dominant and subdominant bucks may begin traveling their rub routes again, usually on their way to and from food sources. They may rub and scrape while

Large rubs like this one may be used most frequently year after year during the pre-primary breeding/scraping phase.

they travel with, or search for, estrus does during the day, especially if there is a full moon. When temperatures are colder than normal daytime activity may occur from two to three hours before sunset to an hour after sunset, and from an hour before sunrise to three to four hours after sunrise.

Late Breeding Phase (Rubbing/Scraping/Searching/Breeding) Dec. 10 to Dec. 25:

Approximately a month after the primary breeding phase unbred older does come into a second estrus. Some 1½-year-old does and 6 of 8 doe fawns come into their first estrus. Dominant and subdominant bucks often travel their rub routes, may make rubs and scrapes, and visit doe-use and feeding areas in their search for receptive does. Daytime activity may occur from two to three hours before sunset to an hour after, and from an hour before sunrise to three to four hours after, especially when the weather is colder than normal and there is cloud cover. I often see dominant and subdominant bucks with the does as they travel to and from food sources during this phase, especially during the full moon.

The neck of this buck is beginning to swell, indicating that it is a breeding buck.

Post-Rut Dec. 25 to Jan. 15: After the rut ends, and when food sources are limited, cold night time and morning temperatures may cause both bucks and does to travel during the afternoon and early evening hours. They may also feed late in the morning when there is prolonged severe weather. My studies show that when the temperature or wind-chill was below 10°F (-12°C), and when there was limited food, three times more deer were sighted in the afternoon and evening than at any other time during the fall. When extreme conditions occur, the moon has very little influence on daytime deer activity.

Biology of the Rut

White-tailed deer use the scent of several different pheromones and hormones along with urine to communicate sexual readiness. In addition, it is believed that several scents associated with buck rubbing and scraping behavior serve to bring the does into estrus. Deer also use these same scents to communicate dominance and use them to locate and track each other.

Deer pheromones, the scents given off by deer, are used as a means of communication. They also serve to stimulate a behavioral response in another animal. White-tailed deer pheromones are present in the forehead, interdigital, tarsal and metatarsal glands. There may also be pheromones associated with the pre-orbital gland and saliva. Many of these scents are used in combination during self-impregnation (rub-urination), and signpost marking (rubbing and scraping) and are interpreted by individual sexes and age classes differently. When used by themselves, these scents may be interpreted differently from when they are used in combination with another scent or scents.

Bucks are able to recognize the scent of other bucks once signpost marking begins. They know which rubs and what overhanging branches at scrapes have been visited by which buck. After being threatened or attacked during the pre-rut and rut, subdominant bucks soon realize they should not be in areas near a dominant buck.

Recognition scents are present all year. They can be used any time during the year or rut without fear of alarming deer. Forehead scent is most prevalent during the rut and is more effective at that time. Because deer are curious about their home range and often exert dominance (even does) in their core area, they may investigate any new scent to find out what deer has been in the area.

Territorial and Dominance Scents

Rubs and scrapes are the dominance areas of mature bucks. These signposts mark the areas used by the buck. Each rub contains scents from the forehead glands. After rubbing, bucks often lick the rubbed tree and because they sometimes lick their own tarsal after rub-urinating there may be urine, testosterone, tarsal and saliva left on the rub. This combination of scents is a territorial signal proclaiming dominance by mature bucks.

These same four scents may occur on the overhanging branch at a scrape along with pre-orbital scents, because the buck sniffs, licks, rubs and chews the branch with his forehead and antlers. Urine, testosterone and tarsal scent are deposited in the scrape during rub-urination. The buck also leaves interdigital scent on the trail of his rub line and in the scrape as he paws the ground. This combination of scents is again a dominance and territorial signal to other bucks and a sign of a mature, dominant, breeding buck to the does.

The complex combination of scents left on signposts occurs primarily during the rut. The scents at the rub occur when bucks begin to shed their velvet. The scents at scrapes begin shortly after rubbing begins, but become most evident about a month later. These scents can be used any time during the rubbing phase to attract bucks, but they become less effective after the first breeding phase. Because a dominant buck makes rubs and scrapes as a prelude to breeding and as a proclamation of dominance, he is impelled to investigate the smell of any unknown buck intruding on his territory.

Estrogen in the urine of a doe signals sexual readiness. Bucks readily respond to estrogen, or other scents that are present when a doe is in heat, soon after they shed their velvet through the second and possibly the third estrus, which may occur as late as January, even in northern latitudes. Because bucks are curious estrogen can be used anytime of the year to attract them.

High amounts of testosterone in urine signal a buck's sexual readiness to does and dominance to other bucks. Testosterone may attract does to a particular area, which in turn attracts bucks. In one study from the University of Georgia, buck urine attracted deer better than estrus urine.

Does travel extensively when they are in heat, often traveling outside their core areas, possibly in search of healthy, dominant bucks to breed with. It has been suggested that does can determine the physical health of the buck by the amount of protein in its urine. The doe chooses the buck she breeds with possibly by the combination of the protein, testosterone and tarsal from rub-urination. I've seen does wait in the vicinity of a scrape of a dominant buck until he showed up.

Miller, Marchinton and Knox presented a scientific paper in 1987, in which they suggested that the scents left behind at rubs may serve as priming pheromones and help bring does into estrus when the does come in contact with the scents. When bucks rub a tree they transfer scents from their sudoriferous (forehead) glands to the tree. The scent from these glands has been correlated with age and probable social status. In other words, does may be able to tell how old a buck is, and probably whether or not it is a dominant buck by the scent it leaves behind at a rub. But, what matters is that when does smell the scents at a rub, it may cause them to come into a silent ovulation. Since rubbing usually peaks early in the rut (mid to late September in many areas), and because the does don't all come in contact with the scents at the rubs at the same time, many of them may come into what deer biologists refer to as a "silent ovulation" or "non-estrus ovulation" in late September and early October, and come into a normal estrus ovulation from late October to late November. During the "silent ovulation" there is not enough estrogen present for the does to conceive. Therefore, the first time they can conceive is during their first "estrus ovulation."

CHAPTER 2

Predicting Deer Activity

While I found the information from my research studies interesting and useful, what I really wanted to know was: What are the best times of the day to hunt trophy-class bucks? I had found no way to predict exactly when trophy bucks would move. What I learned during the study did help me predict the approximate time frames when bucks were most likely to be active. I also learned that those time frames changed as the rut progressed.

One of the things I learned was that deer don't know what time it is. All they know is that it's either getting darker (which means it's safe to go out into the open) or it's getting lighter (which means it's time to head back to the security of their core areas). Since the time of sunrise and sunset changes daily, the best way to predict deer activity is not in relation to the human terms of the hours of a clock, but in relation to the idea of security to a deer. The best way to do that is to tell you when the deer were sighted in relation to sunset and sunrise.

Buck Activity

While long-term deer studies show some of the activity patterns of whitetails during the fall, they do not usually answer the questions hunters want to know most, such as:

- How do different age classes of bucks react during the various phases of the rut?

- Do big bucks react differently than smaller bucks?

- What time of the day are bucks most active?

Some of the answers to those questions were revealed during my studies between 1993 and 2001.

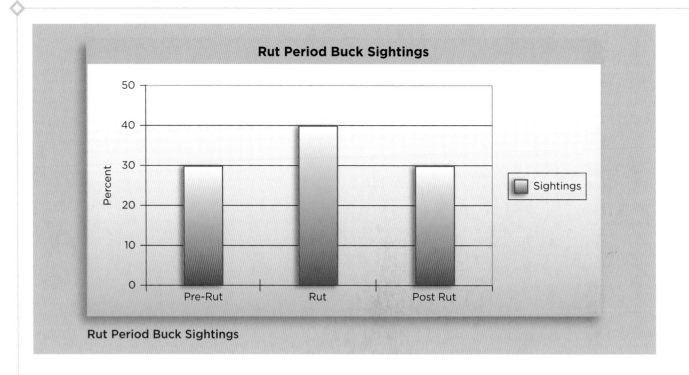

Rut Period Buck Sightings

During 1994, the study was conducted on a deer herd hunted by several archery hunters. I observed the area for 79 days, with 370 hours in the field, from October 1 through January 14. The herd consisted of 33 deer, a 160-class ten-point buck, a 150-class eight-point, a young eleven-point non-typical, a 120-class eight-point, a six-point and two four-point bucks. During the course of the study there were 469 deer sightings.

Throughout the study, bucks were sighted more often in the pre-primary breeding/scraping phase and primary breeding phase of the rut than they were during the pre-rut/rubbing phase or the rest phase. They were again seen in the late breeding phase, when they were frequently seen feeding late in the morning and early in the afternoon.

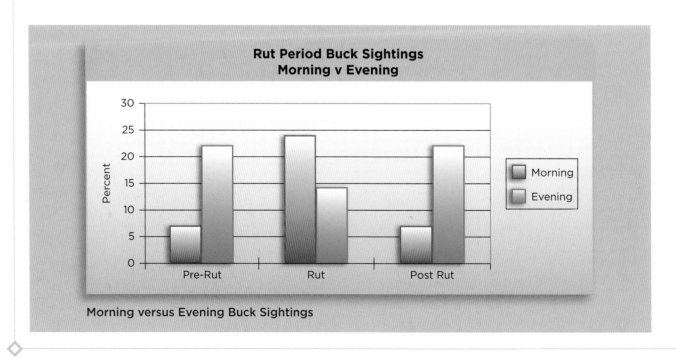

Morning versus Evening Buck Sightings

During my research, the deer were seen outside of their daytime core areas at different times of the day, during the different phases of the rut.

Evening Deer Sightings

Evening doe sightings during the pre-rut/rubbing phase and fall home range shift/dispersal phase occurred from 1 hour before to 1½ hours after sunset, with peak sightings half an hour before sunset and 1 hour after sunset. The sightings of both younger and older bucks occurred and peaked half an hour after sunset.

The pre-primary breeding/scraping phase and primary rut phase evening doe sightings occurred from 2 hours before to half an hour after sunset, with peak sightings half an hour before sunset. The younger buck sightings occurred and peaked half an hour after sunset, older buck sightings occurred from 1½ hours to 1 hour before sunset, with peak sightings about 1 hour before sunset.

The late breeding phase evening doe sightings occurred from 3 hours before to 1 hour after sunset, with peak sightings half an hour after sunset. The younger buck sightings occurred from 1½ hours before to half an hour after sunset, with peak sightings half an hour after sunset; older buck sightings occurred and peaked about half an hour after sunset.

Morning Deer Sightings

The pre-rut phase and fall home range shift/dispersal phase morning doe sightings occurred from half an hour before to 3 hours after sunrise, with peak sightings an hour after sunrise. The younger buck sightings occurred from half an hour before to 1½ after sunrise; with peak sightings half an hour after sunrise, older buck sightings occurred and peaked about half an hour after sunrise.

The pre-primary breeding/scraping phase and primary rut phase morning doe sightings occurred from 1 hour before to 2½ hour after sunrise, with peak sightings half an hour before sunrise and 2½ hours after sunrise. The younger buck sightings occurred from half an hour before to 3 hours after sunrise; with peak sightings half an hour before sunrise, older buck sighting occurred from half an hour before to 2½ hours after sunrise, with peak sightings from half an hour before to half an hour after sunrise.

The late breeding phase morning doe sightings occurred from 1 hour before to 3 hours after sunrise, with peak sightings half an hour after sunrise. Sightings of both subdominant and dominant bucks occurred and peaked half an hour before sunrise.

Throughout the entire rut, bucks were seen one-and-a-half times more often in the evening than they were in the morning. They were sighted three times more often in the morning during the primary breeding phase than during either the pre-rut phase or the post-rut.

This suggests four conclusions. First, that bucks are more active during the pre-primary breeding/scraping phase and primary breeding phase than during the pre-rut/rubbing phase or the rest phase. Second, they are more active during the evening than the morning. Third, they are most active in the morning rather than the evening during the pre-primary breeding/scraping phase and primary breeding phase. And finally, they are more active than normal in the day during the late breeding phase if there are does in estrus, if it is colder than normal for the area, or if food sources are limited. However, these statistics can also be deceiving, because the sightings included both older dominant and younger subdominant bucks.

A look at the results of my studies shows that the sightings of the different age classes of bucks varied by rut phase and that the older and younger bucks moved at different times of the day during the different rut phases. While the sightings of all age classes of bucks combined was highest during the pre-primary breeding/scraping and primary breeding phases, the younger bucks were seen more often in the morning during the pre-primary breeding/scraping and primary breeding phases. The older bucks were seen more often in the evening during the pre-primary breeding/scraping and primary breeding phases.

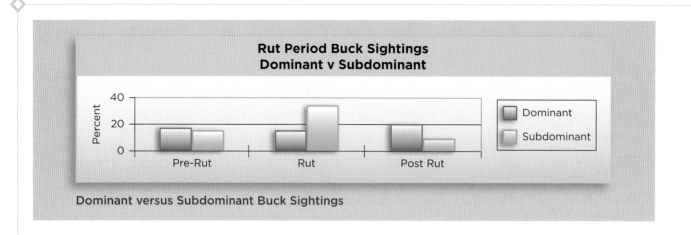

Dominant versus Subdominant Buck Sightings

An even closer look at the studies showed there were distinct differences between the morning and evening sightings of both the older and younger bucks during the different phases of the rut. Overall buck sightings were highest in the evening during all phases of the rut.

The evening sightings of the younger bucks were slightly higher during the pre-primary breeding/scraping phase than during the primary breeding phase or late breeding phase. The evening sightings of the older bucks varied, with 33 percent occurring during the pre-primary breeding/scraping phase, 22 percent during the primary breeding phase, and 45 percent during the late breeding phase. I suspect the older bucks became more active in the evening during the primary breeding phase because the does were in estrus and that the younger subdominants became less active in the evening during the primary breeding phase in an effort to avoid the more aggressive dominant bucks.

The times of my deer sightings coincide with the times when archery hunters most often take bucks. According to the statistics in the twentieth edition of the Pope & Young record book, of the 3,670 heads entered into the book between 1995 and 1996, approximately 20 percent were taken from sunrise to 8 a.m., 20 percent from 8 to 10 a.m., 5 percent from 10 a.m. to noon, less than 5 percent from noon to 2 p.m., 10 percent from 2 to 4 p.m., over 35 percent from 4 to 6 p.m. and over 10 percent from 6 p.m. to sunset.

In a study of radio-collared deer in Texas, Mickey Hellickson found that mature bucks were the least active of all age classes of bucks. Young and middle age bucks were more active and about equal in their daily activity. No reason was given for the difference in activity times between the different age classes of the bucks. However, as a result of my research I believe older bucks have learned to move less to avoid hunters. The activity time for all bucks was lowest from 5 to 6 a.m., and highest from 7 to 8 a.m.. I think that from 5 to 6 a.m. the bucks were probably at food sources and from 7 to 8 a.m. they were probably on their way back to their daytime core areas.

The Moon and Deer Activity

There have been a number of studies and articles recently by researchers and outdoor writers who are trying to determine whether or not there is a correlation between lunar conditions and deer activity. The articles have stirred the interest of whitetail hunters who would like to be able to predict when deer will be seen during the hunting season. Interest in lunar conditions is not new, however; hunters and fisherman have been using the moon to predict game activity for years. This interest in lunar activity and game activity has led to a variety of sun- and moon-related animal activity predictors/tables for hunters and fisherman, and there are more on the way.

Does the Moon Affect Daily Deer Activity?

Several popular game charts claim to be able to predict daily deer activity based on the position of the moon in relation to a given spot on earth.

We know that the gravitational pull of the moon is strongest when the moon is directly overhead and underfoot (directly on the other side of the world), with the greatest gravitational pull often occurring when the moon is directly overhead. This is evidenced by the daily tides, with the highest tide usually occurring when the moon is overhead.

Because the earth revolves as it moves around the sun, the moon will be directly overhead or underfoot at different times each day. The game activity tables take this into account, and predict that deer will be most active or feed when the moon is either directly overhead or underfoot, with predicted major times often coinciding with the overhead position of the moon and minor times coinciding with the underfoot position of the moon.

The Solunar Table, Vektor Fish and Game Activity Tables, Feeding Times and Moon Guide all rely on the position of the moon and claim to be able to predict game activity from a half hour before and after to 2 hours before and after the predicted times. One of them predicts poor, fair good and best days of the month. I placed all these predictor/tables on a graph and found that, because they all rely on lunar orbit, they paralleled each other within hours. However, I noticed that many of the times that they predicted were during the hours of dawn and dusk.

One of the reasons hunters report seeing deer during the times predicted is because the tables predict up to 4 hours each day as the best times to hunt, and they often predict morning and evening times. In November, when there are only about 10 hours of daylight, the chances of seeing deer are obviously fairly high during the predicted times. Because deer are most active in the morning and evening during the fall, and these are the times when most hunters see deer, I decided to check the accuracy of the tables during the predicted midday hours.

The problem with the research, hypotheses, predictors and tables is that there are so many of them and there are so many lunar factors that may or may not influence deer activity. To compound the problem, different researchers use different lunar factors, and combinations of factors, while doing their research and making their predictions, which causes mass confusion among hunters.

At least one outdoor writer claims to have found a correlation between daytime deer activity during specific times of the day and the position of the moon. One researcher claims to have found a correlation between nighttime deer activity and moon phase. Another researcher claims to have found a correlation between monthly daytime deer activity and a combination of lunar factors, which may or may not include the position, amount of light, declination, distance and gravitational pull of the moon. Some of these researchers and writers are currently trying to correlate estrus cycles of white-tailed deer and peak rut activity with moon phase.

Daytime activity, nighttime activity, monthly activity, estrus cycles, peak of the rut, moon phase, moon position, declination, distance, gravity. No wonder it's confusing, and most of it is hypothesis. Even the researchers admit that although they may find a correlation between lunar conditions and deer activity, they are not sure what the causes are.

Contrary to many Game Predictor Tables, peak daytime deer activity does not appear to be correlated with the overhead/underfoot position of the moon.

T.R.'s Test Results

With so many articles being written, so much research being done, and so much hype about how deer react to the varying forces of the moon I decided to test the accuracy of several popular game predictor tables. These tables rely on the position of the moon in relation to a given point on the earth's surface. They predict that game will move and feed at given times of the day (within a two- to five-hour time frame) when the moon is either directly overhead or underfoot. That two- to five-hour time frame covers a fairly large portion of the day and any good hunter should be able to see deer sometime within five hours.

To see how the tables related to each other, I plotted all of the predicted times on a graph. The first thing I noticed was that times predicted by the charts often paralleled each other, but they often predicted game activity at different times each day. I also noticed that many of the predicted activity times coincided with the normal daytime deer activity at dawn and dusk. Obviously hunters would see deer at those times.

I also noticed that the total number of days predicted per month when deer would be seen at dawn or dusk was 25. In other words, the tables predict that deer will move and feed within two to five hours of sunset or sunrise almost every day of the month. But, sunset and sunrise are when deer are most active anyhow.

To find out how well the game activity tables predicted deer activity I kept precise daily records of all my deer sightings from September through January, from 1995 to 2001. To check the accuracy of the tables I chose the month of November, which coincides with the gun season and the rut in many areas. Then I compared the tables with the deer sightings four other hunters and I had. Upon checking the results I found very little correlation between the predictors and deer activity other than during the normal activity times of dawn and dusk.

All the tables predicted game activity during normal morning and evening activity times on five days in November, and above normal deer activity did occur on two of those days. But, the

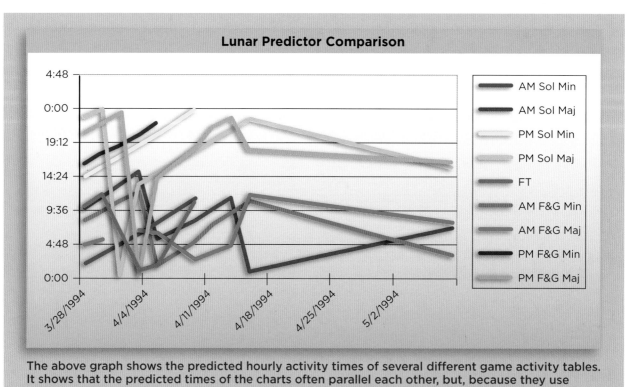

The above graph shows the predicted hourly activity times of several different game activity tables. It shows that the predicted times of the charts often parallel each other, but, because they use different factors associated with the moon, they do not always predict the same hours each day.

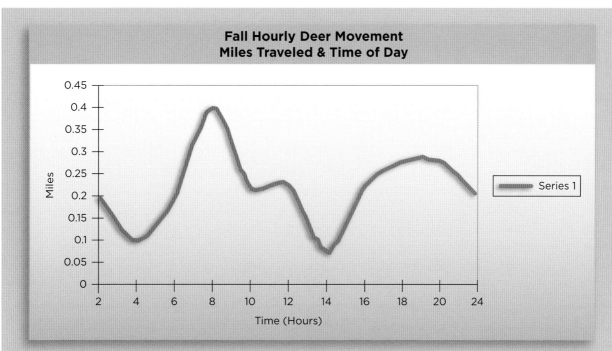

Fall Hourly Deer Movement
Miles Traveled & Time of Day

The above graph shows the hours of the day when deer were most active and how far they may move during those hours. It shows that, instead of deer activity being represented by a fairly straight line from day to day, deer activity generally peaks at sunrise and sunset everyday. Deer activity (or sightings of deer outside of their core areas) rarely peaks between 9 a.m. and 3 p.m., as the lunar predictors suggest.

tables were accurate only 17 percent of the time, and only when they predicted activity during normal deer activity times, in the morning and evening, when hunters see most deer anyhow. There were also four days when above-normal activity occurred when it was not predicted by the tables. Overall the tables did a poor job of accurately predicting hourly deer activity, outside of the normal daily deer activity times of sunset and sunrise.

Because I expected to see deer in the morning and evening I eliminated the hours from sunrise to two hours after sunrise, and from two hours before sunset to sunset. Next I plotted all 102 of my deer sightings for November 1996 on the graph. There were several days when I saw deer at the predicted times, most of them at dawn and dusk. Then, because the tables predicted deer activity during the middle of the day I checked to see how many of the 102 deer sightings occurred during midday. Between 10 a.m. and 3 p.m. there was very little deer activity at the times predicted

by these tables. On several occasions I watched deer lay down and get up, but could not correlate their activity with any of the tables.

I did see a huge eight-point buck on November 15, within the time predicted by all the charts, at 11:15 in the morning. But, it was the peak of the rut, and bucks do stupid things during the rut. The buck was not feeding or going out to feed, it was going back to its core area. It was doing the opposite of what the charts said it should be doing. That was the only one of the 102 deer sightings that occurred at the predicted time. I don't know about other hunters, but a one-percent success rate is not good enough for me. As far as I am concerned these charts don't work. None of the five or six deer researchers I talked to believe these charts work, either.

Research studies of two different deer species, in different years and different locations, show a correlation between deer movement, amount of available lunar light, and lunar orbit, but not with

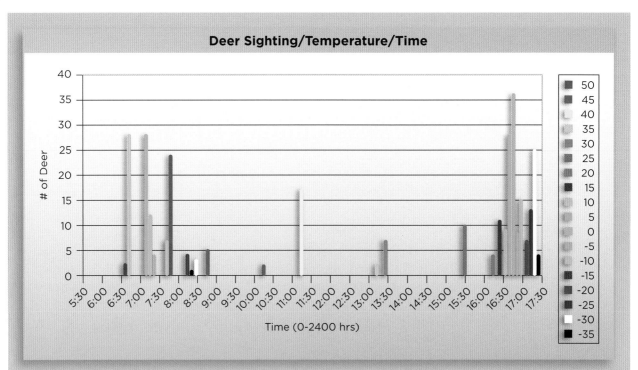

Deer Sighting/Temperature/Time

The graph above shows the number of deer sighted during different times of the day from September 1 through December 31. It clearly shows that most deer sightings occurred between 6:30 and 7:30 a.m. (at the left), and between 4:30 and 5:30 p.m. (at the right). The peak in sightings at 11:00 a.m. occurred when temperatures were below -30°F (-34°C); the deer were seen in brushy areas on the south side of a hill, where they were out of the wind, but could gain some heat through solar radiation. It was obvious they had spent the night near the food sources instead of returning to their normal daytime core areas.

gravitational pull. This clearly shows that game activity tables that rely on the gravitational affect of the moon to predict hourly deer activity do not work.

The problem with using game activity tables is that they don't agree on which days or times of the days are best to hunt. So, which table should you use? Is one better than the others? What if the select days don't coincide with the hunting season, or coincide with the days you have available to hunt? What if the select times don't coincide with the hours you can hunt? Then the tables do you no good. By the way, if you choose to use all the tables available you end up hunting all day, every day for the entire month.

If the game activity tables were correct, then deer sightings should have been equal during all hours of the day, but they weren't. Most deer sightings occurred within one to two hours of sunset and sunrise. This graph clearly shows that game activity tables that rely on the position and/or the gravitational pull of the moon are ineffective at predicting the hours of the day when deer are most active.

The reason these tables are not more accurate is because they cannot take into account all of the other factors that affect daily deer movement: daily meteorological conditions, food availability, the rut, predatory behavior, distance to and from limited/preferred food sources, and hunting pressure. Some weather conditions cause a decrease in daytime deer movement, while other weather conditions cause an increase in daytime deer movement. Abundant food sources often decrease daytime deer movement, while limited food sources often increase daytime deer movement. The rut inevitably increases daytime deer movement. Predatory behavior and hunting pressure reduces daytime deer movement.

When you use lunar predictors without taking into account all of the other factors that cause an increase in daytime deer activity you will inevitably miss some excellent hunting opportunities when above-normal daytime deer activity occurs. If you don't take into account all of the other factors that decrease, and in some cases completely override lunar influence on daytime deer movement, you may hunt several days without seeing a deer. The purpose of a deer activity chart should be to help hunters reliably predict the days when deer will be most active, so they can hunt on those days, and then decide whether or not to hunt the days when deer are not active. And there is a way to do that.

The Daily Deer Movement Indicator

As a result of my four-year study on deer movement, I devised the Daily Deer Movement Indicator (DDMI), which predicts above-normal deer activity based on the time of day, the current weather conditions, moon conditions, the rut and the available food sources. During the same 1994 deer study as mentioned above, the DDMI predicted daytime deer activity on 35 of 60 days.

There was above-normal deer activity on 30 of the 35 days predicted, for an accuracy rate of 86 percent. But, there were two days when above-normal deer activity occurred when it was not predicted.

The DDMI can also be used in conjunction with other predictors. By using the DDMI in combination with a Moon Indicator, the accuracy rate could be increased to 95 percent, almost double the individual accuracy rate. But, there were still those two days when above-normal deer activity occurred when it was not predicted. This only goes to show that there will be times when none of the tables will be accurate in predicting daytime deer activity.

Does The Moon Affect Monthly Deer Activity?

As I mentioned before, there are also hypotheses that the moon affects monthly deer activity. Like other hunters, I wanted to know if the hypotheses were reliable. So, I checked to see what other writers and researchers thought. There seems to be a difference of opinion.

Most daytime deer activity occurs in secure areas, such as this heavily wooded area, which is probably in the deer's daytime core area.

Studies suggest that deer, including dominant bucks, are more active during daylight hours when the moon is in the full or last quarter phase.

One writer says moon phases should be ignored. Another says those who ignore moon phases should spend more time in the deer forest and less time in the library. Still another says that moon phases might have some effect, but there are too many other conflicting factors (such as weather and hunting pressure) to sort it all out. The last writer is closest to the truth. Daytime deer activity is governed by the weather, food availability, the rut, hunting pressure, and the moon.

Fall deer activity occurs primarily during low light conditions, and anything that alters the available amount of light also affects deer movement, especially during the hours of dawn and dusk. The moon reflects enough light when the sky is clear that I believe it causes decreased deer activity at dawn and dusk. Noted wildlife researcher, Dr. Valerius Geist, agrees with me, and says he sees fewer deer during dawn and dusk when there is abundant moonlight.

In his study on white-tailed deer, Kammermeyer found that deer activity was greater in both daylight and dark hours when the moon was in the light phase (greater than half moon) than it was during the dark phase (less than half moon). He also found that deer activity was significantly greater during the day between the hours of 8 and 10 a.m., during the full moon phase.

In a study of sambar deer in Florida, Lewis, Flynn, R.L. Marchinton, Shea and E.M. Marchinton also found greater deer activity from moonrise to moonset during the full moon than in the new moon phase. No correlation of sambar deer movement with tidal activity was noted, which suggests that the moon's gravitational forces were not directly responsible for any effect the moon may have on deer movement. It was noted that the greatest monthly movement of the sambar deer occurred during the seven days before the perigee of the moon.

The orbit of the moon is elliptical, not round. And it is not centered on the earth, it is lopsided. The perigee occurs when the moon is at its closest distance from the earth, about 221,463 miles (354,340 km). The apogee occurs when the moon is at its farthest distance from the earth, about 252,710 miles (404,336 km). As the moon approaches the perigee it begins to speed up due to the increase in the gravitational pull of the earth. This increase in speed occurs during the week before the perigee. The week before the perigee is when the moon's acceleration is greatest in its elliptical orbit. Researcher G. L. Plummer suggests that "biomagnetics" (the biological responses to changes in the physical properties of magnetism) associated with the moon's acceleration during the perigee could possibly affect deer movement. The apogee of the moon may also affect biomagnetics and deer activity.

There are several individual lunar factors that may affect daily and monthly deer movement and it appears that researchers have found correlations between some of these individual factors, or combinations of individual factors, and deer activity during different times of the day and night, even if they are not sure what causes these correlations. The researchers also agree that the accuracy of lunar predictor tables can be greatly affected by several other factors including weather, the rut and the availability of food.

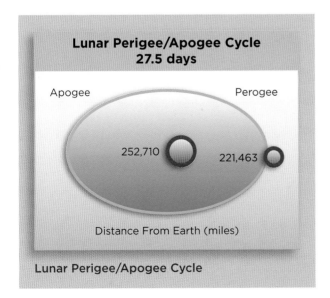

**Lunar Perigee/Apogee Cycle
27.5 days**

Apogee

Perogee

252,710

221,463

Distance From Earth (miles)

Lunar Perigee/Apogee Cycle

The problem with predicting peak monthly daytime deer activity is that it appears that the full moon, perigee and apogee all affect deer movement, and that peak monthly activity may occur during the coincidence of the full moon and the perigee or apogee. But there are variances in when the full moon, the perigee and the apogee occur. The lunar phase cycle and the lunar perigee/apogee cycle are on two different time frames. While the full moon occurs approximately every 29.5 days as it revolves around the earth in relation to the sun, the lunar perigee/apogee cycle occurs approximately every 27.5 days, therefore, the perigee and apogee occur about 14 days apart. As a result of this difference in the two cycles, the full moon and the perigee/apogee can occur on the same day (as they did on September 16, 1997), or they can occur as much as two weeks apart.

One reason why deer may be more active during the day when the full moon, perigee or apogee occur may be due to predatory behavior. If wolves, bears, coyotes and so on are more active during the full moon, the perigee or the apogee, deer may be forced to become more active in their efforts to avoid the predators. If predatory behavior occurs at night, during the full moon, when the predators can easily see, the deer may not be able to eat as much as normal. Consequently, they may be conditioned to search more for food in the daytime during a full moon, the perigee or the apogee.

The Moon Indicator

To see if my 1999 assumptions about the full moon and perigee/apogee held up I checked them with my deer sightings from 1994 to 1997. Plotting both the perigee/apogee and the full moon on a graph, and then plotting the daily deer sightings, I found that peak monthly daytime deer sightings did occur during the full moon.

As a result of my research, I devised the Moon Indicator (MI), which helps predict peak monthly deer activity. Although the MI is quite effective in September, October, December, January and February, it does poorly during November when the rut is on. This is owing to generally increased deer activity throughout the month, which results in no noticeable peak in daytime deer activity.

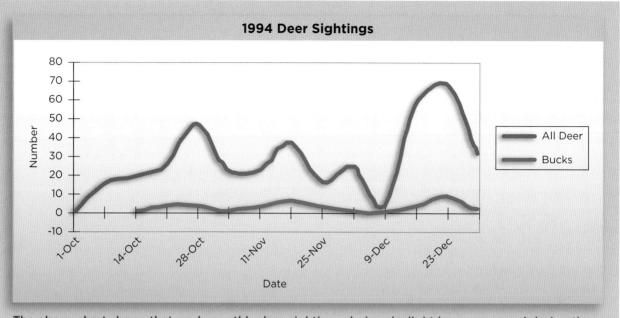

1994 Deer Sightings

The above chart shows that peak monthly deer sightings during daylight hours occurred during the full and last quarter of the moon, with peak sightings during the full moon.

The MI also does not work well anytime the hunting season is in progress (no matter what month), because hunting pressure causes a decrease in daytime deer activity. It is also not effective when daily meteorological conditions are severe, because severe weather causes a decrease in daytime deer movement. However, the MI can be very effective during the late season when food sources are low, because low food sources and cold weather cause an increase in daytime deer activity as the deer search for food.

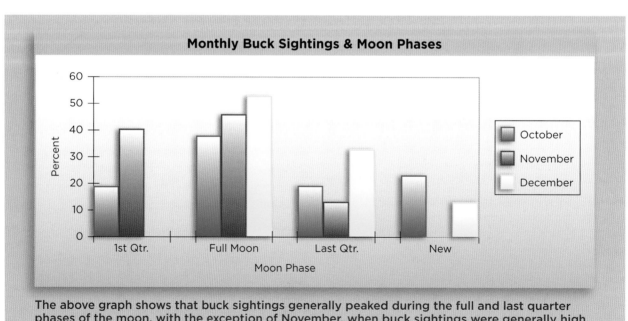

Monthly Buck Sightings & Moon Phases

The above graph shows that buck sightings generally peaked during the full and last quarter phases of the moon, with the exception of November, when buck sightings were generally high throughout the month due to breeding readiness of the does.

It appears that peak monthly daytime deer activity, including that of dominant bucks, occurs when there is a coincidence of the full moon and the perigee/apogee. Both bucks and does can be expected to move throughout the day during this time. However, this activity is greatly affected by several other factors, particularly food availability, meteorological conditions, the rut and hunting pressure. My research also shows that most of the daytime activity of dominant bucks will still occur at dawn and dusk, even during the rut.

Lunar Factors and the Rut

Several outdoor writers believe they have found a way to predict the peak of the rut by using moon phases. One writer believes that the rut will begin five to seven days after the second full moon after the fall equinox, which occurs on September 21 or 22. He believes that the peak of the rut will occur during the new moon. Two others believe the rut will peak during the full moon and last quarter of the moon. Another writer believes that the peak of the rut will occur five to seven days before the first new moon following the second full moon after the fall equinox. What they are all saying is that peak breeding will occur somewhere between the full moon and the following new moon. That would mean the peak of the rut would normally occur before the new moon in November.

There are several reasons why the "five to seven days before the new moon" theory may not hold up. The main reason is because the study was based in part on a study of water buffalo in India. While the theory may apply to water buffalo in India, deer biologists are quick to point out that water buffalo are not deer, but a form of cattle. Several researchers also point out that the tropical weather conditions in India are far different from the temperate conditions of North America.

There are basic problems with these hypotheses. One is that they have not been thoroughly tested or proven yet. Another is that they each predict a slightly different time frame. One theory suggests that the peak of the rut will occur before the new moon, one suggests that the peak will occur during the full moon and last quarter, and yet another suggests that the peak of the rut will occur five to seven days before the new moon. They can't all be right, yet it would be hard to say that any of them are wrong, because peak breeding in many areas usually lasts from two to three weeks. The chances are those two to three weeks would include portions of both the full moon and the new moon, and everything in between.

Breeding Activity

One thing that must be made clear is that all of the breeding activity does not occur during the one week of the peak of the rut. Larry Marchinton's studies in Georgia, and my own studies in Minnesota, show that the breeding season often lasts 60 days or more. While the peak of the rut may occur in November, these studies show that from 10 to 20 percent of the does may be bred in October, 40 to 60 percent in November and another 20 to 30 percent in December, depending on the area, buck-to-doe ratio, the health of the deer, and the age structure of the herd. In Marchinton's study the 1½-year-old does came into their first estrus in October and November. In most northern areas half-year-old does come into their first estrus in December. Generally speaking, in northern areas, the November primary rut will last three weeks, with the peak of the breeding occurring from 1½ to two weeks after the first doe comes into estrus in mid-November.

The hypothesis about breeding activity and the phase of the moon involve lunar light, melatonin and reproductive hormones. Melatonin is believed to be a regulator of hormones, and as such it may have the ability to affect the growth and shedding of hair, and affect estrus cycles. It is believed that melatonin is produced during the dark. Because melatonin regulates the production of hormones, some of the writers/researchers feel that a reduction in melatonin during the full moon triggers breeding activity. Supposedly, it takes a few days for the reduction in melatonin levels and the corresponding rise in reproductive hormone levels to occur. Then, supposedly, peak breeding activity occurs five to seven days after

Conclusive research studies have shown that peak breeding of whitetails is not affected by or correlated with the full moon, or any other phase of the moon.

These hypotheses may be based, in part, on the misconception that the estrus cycle of whitetails occurs every 28 days, which coincides with a 28-day lunar cycle. However, neither the moon nor a whitetail has a 28-day cycle. It actually takes the moon 29 days, 12 hours, 44 minutes and 2.8 seconds to orbit the earth once, and not all whitetails come into estrus every 28 days. Studies by Dr. Larry Marchinton in Georgia show that does come into estrus from 21 to 30 days, not every 28 days as previously thought. Therefore, even if the first estrus of a doe fell on a specific moon phase during one month, the second estrus could be as much as a week before the same moon phase a month later. I mention the first estrus because several studies on white-tailed deer and other hoofed animals suggest that females experience a non-estrus ovulation approximately 12 to 23 days prior to having their first estrus ovulation. If this is true, and the moon phase does affect the estrus cycle of deer, then the first "estrus" of the doe may not occur during the same moon phase a month later, because the doe may not come into estrus exactly 28 days later.

During the non-estrus ovulation the does ovulate, but there are not enough reproductive hormones present for the doe to conceive and become pregnant. What this means is that, if the moon does influence breeding behavior, and the moon does affect the estrus cycle of the doe, it is the moon phase the month before the doe comes into estrus that starts the process, and there is the crux of the problem.

Let's suppose that the full moon does trigger a reduction in melatonin level, which in turn triggers the first ovulation cycle of the doe (five to seven days after the full moon). In much of North America, white-tailed does are bred in November. That would mean that it was the full moon in October that triggered the ovulation cycle. Remember, does do not come into a first "estrus" ovulation until 12 to 23 days after their "silent" ovulation. And we have to add five to seven days for the "melatonin effect" to the 12 to 23 days between the silent ovulation and estrus ovulation.

the full moon. However, the effects of low light conditions that affect the rutting period of white-tailed deer are thought to be in relation to the reduction of solar light, or daily photoperiod, during the fall, not the increase of lunar light.

To check the validity of this theory I spoke to several well-respected deer researchers. Dr. Valerius Geist does not believe there is a correlation between melatonin, moon phase and estrus cycles. He doesn't believe there is enough light during the full moon to affect overall monthly melatonin production. He also agrees that the prevalence of clouds during the fall would eliminate most of the lunar light during the full moon. Dr. Karl Miller does not believe there is a correlation between moon phase and whitetail estrus cycles either. He told me that in their tests with melatonin, the deer grew winter coats earlier than they normally would, but the average first estrus dates did not change. This suggests that melatonin is not the only thing that controls estrus dates.

What that means is: If a doe experienced a non-estrus ovulation five to seven days after the October full moon, and if she experienced an estrus ovulation 23 days after her non-estrus ovulation, she could come into estrus during the November full moon. But, what if she comes into an estrus ovulation 12 days after her non-estrus ovulation? Then she would come into estrus nine days before the full moon. Now remember that the moon hypothesis suggest the doe will come into estrus from five days before to nine days after the full moon. It just doesn't add up.

T.R.'S KEYPOINTS

Breeding behavior causes bucks to establish and maintain dominance. Their movements are influenced by the urge to make rubs and scrapes in doe-use areas, and to find does. They travel from one dominance area to the next. These dominance areas usually coincide with individual doe areas and food sources.

Bucks encountering estrus does may stop traveling their routes for up to 48 hours to follow the does. Bucks may be late returning to their beds the next day and rest a day before returning to normal activities.

The farther away, less comfortable, less secure, more pressured and more interested in breeding deer are, the longer it may take them to arrive at openings and food sources at night, and the later they may return to their core areas in the morning.

Breeding urges may cause bucks to move earlier than normal in the evening during the rut. Deer may be seen in the later afternoon/early evening in travel corridors and along rub routes.

During the rut, bucks travel in almost any weather condition to find does, even extreme weather as does remain in core areas and are easily found.

The Full Moon and Rut Synchronization

I've already mentioned that does experience a non-estrus ovulation prior to having a normal estrus ovulation, which is when they can normally be expected to breed and conceive. And I mentioned that it appears there is no correlation between the phase of the moon and peak breeding. We do know that it is the shortening number of hours of light each day that triggers the rut. But is there anything besides the sun that helps ensure that bucks and does are ready to breed at the same time?

As I stated earlier, Miller, Marchinton and Knox presented a scientific paper in 1987, in which they suggested that the scents left behind at rubs may serve as priming pheromones to help bring does into estrus when the does come in contact with the scents. When bucks rub a tree they transfer scents from their sudoriferous (forehead) glands to the tree. The scent from these glands has been correlated with a buck's age and probable social status. In other words, does may be able to tell how old a buck is, and probably whether or not it is a dominant buck or not, by the scent it leaves behind at a rub. But, what matters is, that when does smell the scents at a rub it may cause them to come into a non-estrus. Since rubbing usually peaks early in the rut (mid to late September in many areas), and because the does don't all come in contact with the scents at the rubs at the same time, many of them may come into a non-estrus ovulation in late September or early October and come into a normal estrus ovulation from late October to late November.

Interestingly, during Marchinton's 1985 study, the full moon occurred on October 28 and again on November 27, with peak estrus occurring November 9, showing no correlation with the full moon. This lack of a correlation between moon phase and peak rut was to be expected because of the lateness of the November full moon. I suspect that when the full moon occurs too early or too late the rut will occur when it usually does, during mid November in the many areas.

Even if the amount of moonlight would cause does to come into estrus, Marchinton's research shows that not all does come into estrus during a particular moon phase, or even during the same month. As mentioned earlier, Marchinton found that the estrus cycles of does ranged from 21 to 30 days, with an average of 26 days, but the moon phase changes every 29½ days. Therefore, if a doe came into estrus during the full moon in October, and assuming it wasn't bred, its second estrus could occur as much as a week before the full moon in November and two weeks before the full moon in December.

My studies, research by Kent Kammermeyer, and research by Grant Woods, suggest there is a correlation between increased daytime deer activity and the moon. These correlations are related to the position of the moon and the earth, the distance of the moon from the earth, the position and speed of the moon in its elliptical orbit, and combinations of these factors. The position of the moon (not the amount of light) during the full moon phase may cause increased gravitational pull, the distance and acceleration of the moon during the perigee (when it is closest to the earth in its elliptical orbit) may cause changes in magnetics. The independent or combined effects of these two factors appear to increase daytime deer activity.

Because the perogee/apogee cycle of the moon has a 27½ day cycle, and the light phase of the

moon has a 29½ day cycle, the full moon and the perigee can occur on the same day, or as much as two weeks apart. This difference in cycle lengths may be the reason why deer activity is high during the full moon in some years but not in others. I suspect that when the full moon and the perigee occur at about the same time (as in 1997) it may cause increased daytime deer activity.

No one really knows how these lunar factors affect deer activity, which lunar factors influence deer activity and how much, or what happens when the perigee and the full moon occur two weeks apart. The key thing to remember is that daytime deer activity (including breeding-related activity) appears to be highest during the week of the full moon each month. However, hunting pressure, the rut, food availability and the weather can completely override any effect the moon has on deer. My studies show that during November, when both the hunting season and rut are in progress, there was no noticeable peak in daytime deer activity.

Even though we may not be able to predict when peak breeding occurs, there appears to be a correlation between lunar factors and daytime

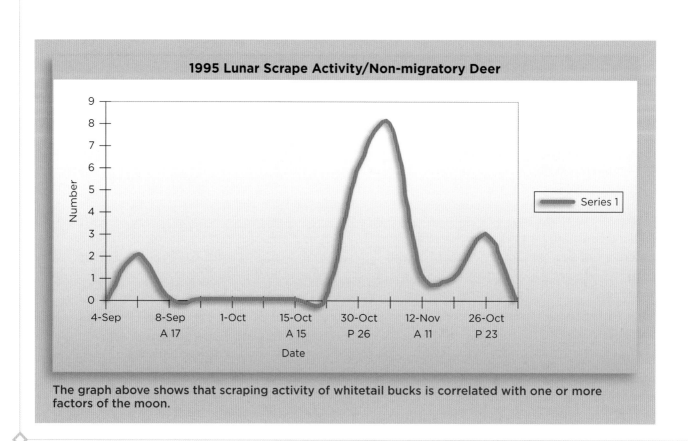

The graph above shows that scraping activity of whitetail bucks is correlated with one or more factors of the moon.

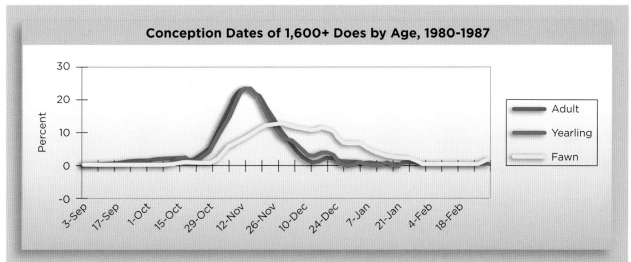

Conception Dates of 1,600+ Does by Age, 1980-1987

This graph of conception dates of whitetail does in Minnesota, from 1980 to 1987, shows that peak breeding in Minnesota occurs during the second week of November, every year, regardless of the moon phase. Note: Data provided by the MN Department of Natural Resources

deer activity. When normal deer activity, caused by the weather, the rut, or lunar factors, occurs during the day, you would expect that rut-related activities such as rubbing, scraping and breeding would also occur during the day. Because Dr. Grant Woods has researched several other deer activities I asked him if this assumption was true. He states that when lunar forces cause increased daytime deer activity you can also expect rut activity, including rubbing, scraping and breeding, to occur during the day. Incidentally, I found that the Moon Indicator is fairly accurate at predicting when peak scrape activity will occur.

Regional Rut Differences

Since deer inhabit much of North America and climatic conditions differ substantially from area to area, their breeding dates adapt to correspond with the best time for fawn survival in their area. As a result of this, peak breeding may occur as early as the first week of November in the North, and as late as January in the south. It may vary by as much as a month for different deer herds in the same state.

It is this variability of the rut in different areas that causes the differing opinions on whether or not the moon influences deer activity during the rut. Let's assume that peak breeding in Minnesota

occurs during mid November, and that peak breeding in west Texas occurs during the first week of December (which is when researchers say peak rut occurs in those areas). When the new moon occurs in mid November the hunters in Minnesota report seeing a lot of breeding activity during the new moon. But the hunters in west Texas report seeing very little breeding activity during the new moon, because peak breeding in west Texas occurs two weeks later, during the full moon.

In order for researchers to feel confident of their findings they need data on hundreds of deer over several years. While the results of these long-term studies may show significant differences in deer activity, they often do not reflect the daily or monthly activity that hunters see, because most hunters do not sight enough deer in a season to notice differences in activity patterns. My records indicate that monthly daytime deer activity peaks during October and December, but may not show a noticeable peak in November, when either the rut or the hunting season is in progress.

While some researchers and writers claim that peak breeding activity will occur during particular moon phases, these phases don't occur at the same time each year. In 1994 the full moon occurred on November 19. My records indicate

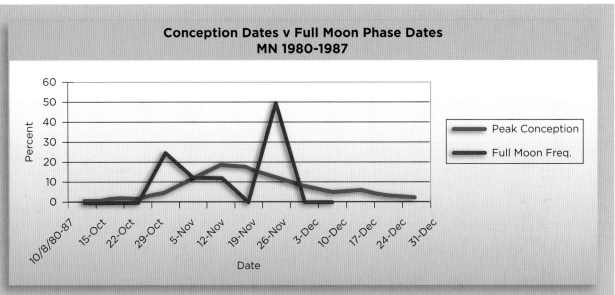

Conception Dates v Full Moon Phase Dates
MN 1980-1987

The graph above shows the relationship between peak conception dates from 1980 to 1987, and when full moon dates occurred during those years. It reveals no correlation between peak breeding and the full moon. It shows that even though the full moon occurred most frequently during the last week of October and the last week of November between 1980 and 1987, peak breeding occurred most frequently during the second week of November, which was either two weeks after or two weeks before the full moon.

that peak breeding behavior in my area occurred November 17. In 1996 the new moon occurred on November 11 and the full moon occurred on November 25. My records indicate that peak breeding behavior occurred on November 15. In 1997 the new moon occurred on October 31 and November 30, with a full moon on November 14. My records indicate that peak breeding behavior occurred on November 16, not the end of October or the end of November. This shows that peak breeding occurs in mid November no matter what the moon phase is, at least in my area. The data from my studies and the studies of other researchers indicate increased daytime deer activity during the rut from approximately a week before to a week after the peak of the rut, no matter what the moon phase is.

The Conception Dates chart clearly shows that the Moon Phase-Peak Breeding Hypothesis of white-tailed deer does not hold up. Because the moon phases change each year, we would expect that a graph of breeding dates over an eight-year period would either have several small peaks, or a small curve, instead of a very noticeable spike.

The noticeable spike on this graph convincingly shows that peak breeding during the eight years of this study always occurred during the second week of November, which completely disproves the Moon Phase-Peak Breeding Hypothesis.

During my research I did see increased daytime breeding activity when particular lunar factors occurred during the time when peak breeding normally occurred. As a result of this I devised my Rut Indicator, which predicts the dates each year when hunters can expect to see the most daytime activity of bucks during the rut. The dates when hunters are most likely to see daytime rut activity, including chasing and breeding, are the dates when the peak of the rut in each area are the same as the dates given on the Rut Indicator.

My records indicate that you can expect to see peak deer sightings during October and December as a result of lunar factors, but you may not see a noticeable peak in deer activity in November, when either the rut or the hunting season is in progress. This is because breeding behavior often increases daytime deer activity during the rut, and hunting often decreases daytime deer activity during the hunting season. The result is that daytime deer activity and sightings remain fairly constant throughout the month, especially when both the rut and the hunting season are in progress at the same time.

Because it appears that some factors associated with the moon do affect daily deer activity, hunters may see more bucks in daylight hours during peak breeding. They may also see fewer bucks depending on when those lunar factors occur, what the buck-to-doe ratio in the area is, the ages of the bucks in the area, and the quality of the habitat. If the buck-to-doe ratio is high they may see lots of bucks competing for the does. If the buck ratio is low they may see fewer bucks, because the few bucks there are may stay near the does for up to three days while they are in heat. If most of the bucks are 3 years old, hunters may see more bucks chasing does and fighting than if there are mostly 2-year-old and younger bucks (as is the case in many areas). This is because younger bucks are less likely to rub, scrape and be aggressive when there are older bucks in the area. In areas of poor habitat (such as large coniferous wooded areas and prairies) hunters may see very few bucks in any one area, because the bucks have to travel extensively to find food and does.

The timing of the rut in much of North America is often correlated with spring temperatures warm enough that the fawns won't die of exposure.

Moon Influence Conclusions

What this means is that, during the fall, and during the rut, hunters can expect bucks to be more active in the day than normal during the week of the full moon, because the full moon does appear to cause deer (including trophy class bucks) to become more active than normal during the week it occurs. This may be especially true if the week of the full moon coincides with peak scraping, or with the peak of the rut (peak breeding), when the bucks are most likely to be active and aggressive. Hunters should remember that the "cumulative" effects of the different factors of the moon might occur from 1 to 3 days after the full moon the farther north the deer are.

Hunters should not rely on the Hourly Game Activity tables to tell them what hours of the day to hunt, because scientific studies have shown that deer movement is not affected by the overhead or underfoot position of the moon. They also should not rely on any moon-based Peak Breeding Dates chart or Rut Dates table that predicts when the peak of the whitetail rut will occur, because the scientific studies show that there is no correlation between any moon phase and peak breeding of white-tailed deer. Research has clearly shown that peak breeding of whitetails occurs on different dates in different states. Sometimes it occurs on different dates in different areas of the same state. Therefore, Peak Breeding Dates charts or Rut Dates tables that use the moon in their predictions cannot possibly predict peak breeding in all of the areas of North America.

Now, I'm going to stretch things a little. During my research in Minnesota, I have found that the rubbing and scraping of white-tailed bucks was correlated with several different lunar factors, one of them being the full moon phase. If peak rubbing is correlated with the full moon, and if does come into a non-estrus ovulation a few days later (say five to seven days) as a result of coming into contact with priming pheromones at rubs, then there might be a correlation with the non-estrus ovulation of a doe and the moon. But that does not mean that there will be a correlation with peak breeding and the moon, because the does don't all come into a normal estrus 28 days later. They may come into a normal first estrus from 12 to 23 days later. This could result in most of the breeding occurring from mid October to late November in many areas, which it does.

The statements of two outdoor writers who promote the peak breeding/moon phase theory need to be clarified. The first statement is that the buck harvest statistics from Illinois support the new moon/peak breeding theory. This is wrong. Buck harvest statistics prove only that bucks were active or vulnerable at that time. If anything, high buck-hunting success rates support the idea that bucks move a lot to avoid hunters when there are many hunters in the woods. It also supports the idea that deer (including bucks) are often most active in daylight hours during the full and last quarter phases of the moon.

The other statement, which I paraphrase, was "an indication that breeding is over, is when scraping stops." My seven-year scrape study and the studies of other researchers, shows that a dramatic reduction in scraping in November often coincides with peak breeding. In other words, a decrease in scraping activity often signals that peak breeding is in progress. I won't argue the idea that a complete cessation of scraping is a good indicator that most of the breeding is over, but a complete cessation in breeding doesn't usually occur until December in many areas.

Seasonal Changes and Deer Activity

Several different factors determine when and where deer move during the fall. An understanding of these factors can explain the reduced sightings of bucks during the hunting season. These factors fall into seven different categories: comfort, security, predatory behavior (natural predators and hunting), food availability, travel distance, breeding behavior and lunar factors.

Fall signals an increase in white-tailed deer activity, which is brought on by changing food supplies

As the does start coming into estrus bucks begin to move more during daylight hours than normal.

and the rut. In a study by Kammermeyer and Marchinton, deer traveled greater average distances per day during the fall than they did in the summer. The deer also traveled greater distances per hour during both dawn and dusk in the fall than during the summer. The researchers also saw a shift in daytime deer activity. During the day in the summer, the deer were most active at dusk, from 6 to 10 p.m. During the day in the fall, they were most active at dawn, from 4 to 10 a.m., with activity continuing until noon.

Overall, the deer were more active during darkness in the fall than they were in the summer. This increase in activity can be attributed to decreased hours of daylight (in some areas from 14 to 8 hours), decreased foliage as leaves fell (leaving deer more exposed during daylight hours) and a change in food sources. During the summer, deer can feed securely in wooded areas where there is abundant forage. In the fall, deer often feed more heavily on agricultural crops, and browse in more open areas, which causes more nighttime feeding. The change in feeding patterns, from wooded areas in the summer to open food sources in the fall, forces the deer to travel farther in search of food. I refer to this deer movement from bedding sites to food sources as the distance factor.

In most areas inhabited by whitetails, fall brings significant changes in weather patterns. Barometric pressure and temperatures fluctuate more, there is more cloud cover, more precipitation and stronger winds. These changes often combine to create low temperatures, changes in dewpoint, lower wind-chill factors and storms. These meteorological changes create a reduction in plant chlorophyll production, causing some plant food sources to die or become dormant, leaves to fall, and other food sources to ripen.

As fall approaches and deer begin growing heavy winter coats, the temperature, precipitation, humidity, wind, dewpoint, wind-chill, and amount of vegetation and cloud cover all affect the comfort of the deer. I refer to these meteorological changes as comfort factors. In extreme conditions meteorological changes may also affect the

health of the deer, and as such they can also be considered as security factors.

Deer activity is governed to a great extent by the availability of food. As food sources become depleted in the fall, deer are forced to travel greater distances. They often shift their feeding patterns to take advantage of foods that ripen or become available during the fall. Depending on how scattered these available food sources are, and how close they are to individual deer core areas, the deer may move more, or less, than normal. This distance factor is directly linked to the food factor and these two together, because of their importance to deer survival, can affect how much time is devoted to other fall deer activities.

The availability of food sources may have a significant effect on dominant buck activity during the rut. Miller reported less rubbing activity by bucks during a year when there was low oak mast (acorn) production. The reduction in rubbing activity may have occurred because the bucks spent more time in search of food and therefore had less time available for rubbing behavior. This could lead to fewer buck sightings near traditional rub routes and scrapes during years of low mast production.

Fewer buck sightings during the fall can also be attributed to the increased size of home ranges during the season. This occurs when bucks begin traveling farther from their seasonal core areas in the fall as they search for new food sources and does to breed. During a study by Kammermeyer and Marchinton the average range of bucks increased from 170 acres (71 ha) in the summer to 310 acres (124 ha) in the fall. During my study in Minnesota, the range of bucks increased from 300 to 1,500 acres (120 to 600 ha). The average daily distance traveled by bucks may also increase during the rut. Bucks in the boreal forest of eastern Canada commonly travel 20 to 25 miles (32 to 40 km) every five to seven days in search of does. The combination of this breeding factor, and the need to find food causes increased buck movements, and, depending on the amount of distance traveled and the time deer spend in specific locations, can lead to fewer buck sightings.

CHAPTER 3

Reading Whitetail Sign

Reading sign helps you determine which areas the deer are using and when they are using them. Determining when the deer use particular areas is the key to knowing where to set up during the hunting season.

Trails

One of the most visible big game signs is trails, and being able to interpret trails can tell you where and when to find game. While most hunters know that big game animals prefer to travel into the wind they don't take wind into account when reading sign. If the game prefers to travel into the wind, their trails should reflect the prevailing wind direction.

I have kept a daily record of wind direction and speed from September through December. Looking at the data I found that out of 102 sightings of deer or deer groups, 64 percent of the movement was into the wind, with 60 percent of the movement in a westerly direction. That may not sound like much until you realize that 84 percent of the total movement was either westerly or into the wind. In my area, the wind is primarily out of the west during the fall. In the particular area of this study, the food sources were west of most of the deer core areas, therefore much of the movement I saw was in a westerly direction. But at what time of day did the deer move? My data shows that the deer traveled west 79 percent of the time in the evening, and east 67 percent of the time in the morning. They moved west to food sources in the evening and east to their core areas in the morning. When you are reading sign, remember that the availability of preferred food has a strong influence on game movement and should be taken into account. The pattern I saw may not occur in other areas. But, if you keep a journal of deer activity in your area, the local patterns will become evident.

In hilly or mountainous regions deer, elk and other animals take advantage of thermal currents. Thermals rise in the morning and fall in the evening. By bedding high during the day they can catch uphill scents. By moving downhill in the evening they move into the thermals that are still rising. Game animals often bed low at night where they catch any falling scent with the changing thermals. When they move uphill to beds in the morning, they move into thermals that are still falling. When you are scouting and observing, and see trails, tracks, droppings, rubs, scrapes and beds in certain areas, and you understand how the animals react to the wind and thermal currents, you are better able to interpret sign correctly. This helps reduce the time needed to locate the game.

The purpose of a trail is to get the animals from one high-use area to another. The preference of the animal is to travel through the areas of least resistance, so they expend the least amount of energy. The preference of the animal to move through the area of least resistance is overridden by the need for security. Security to a prey species like deer is being in a place where it cannot see, smell or hear a predator. With sight a primary means of detection, deer prefer to move when and where they cannot be seen or they cannot see predators.

Trails used at night, when animals feel secure under the cover of darkness, are often located in open fields, on hilltops and in meadows. These are areas the animals wouldn't use during the day because of the exposure. Daytime trails are usually located in woods, brush, heavy cover, ravines, gullies or low-lying routes, where visibility is limited. Traveling low routes has other advantages. Winds are not as strong in low areas as they are at higher elevations, which results in less noise. Scents may gather in low areas where they are not easily dispersed by winds. Traveling in low-lying routes allows animals be relatively unseen, to smell any scents left by predators, and to be able to hear more than in more exposed areas.

Groups of trails and hubs are found in high-use areas at bottlenecks adjacent to preferred travel routes, crossings, staging areas, food sources, bedding sites and watering areas. The amount of cover dictates when these areas are used. Groups of trails that join in wooded areas usually indicate daytime staging or core areas, or food and water sources. Groups of trails that join in open areas indicate nighttime bedding sites or food and water sources. Groups of trails may mean regular use by both does and bucks on different trails. They may also indicate areas where the game moves deeper into cover once vegetation is gone. Hubs (several trails that cross each other) are usually found where different groups of animals travel from one high use area to another.

The frequency of use of the trail can be judged by the amount of vegetation or snow in the trail, or the relative number of tracks. The less vegetation or snow, and the more tracks, the more the trail is used. I check a trail after it has rained or snowed to find out how many tracks there are, and to see if it has been recently used. I often kick dirt, leaves or snow over the existing tracks, and then check them later. I also use a Trail Timer to see how many animals use the trail, and when they use it.

Correctly reading and interpreting whitetail sign, to determine the best times and place to hunt, can lead you to mature, trophy-class bucks.

Drag marks of the front hooves in shallow snow often indicates that a buck made the tracks.

Frequent use of a trail can tell you how often (and sometimes how many) animals use the trail, but may not indicate the type or importance of the trail. Traditional trails, those that are used year after year, may show little use during certain seasons. Trails leading to ripening agricultural crops may only be used in the fall and winter. Less frequently used trails may be used only at certain times of the year, certain times of the day, or used for escape. They may also be used by only one doe group, or one buck. Infrequently used trails that parallel more heavily used trails, or are in heavier cover, when used by only one animal, indicate a buck trail. The presence of other sex-related sign (tracks, drag marks, clumped droppings) should be looked for to confirm that it is a buck trail. If you find rubs and scrapes, you have found a rub route.

Locating frequently used trails is the key to locating the high-use areas of the animals and setting up in the right spot at the right time for hunting. If you find the does you will find the bucks during the rut. Locating buck trails, especially rub routes, is the key to locating the buck's high-use areas, which is the key to hunting bucks.

Tracks

Tracks can help you determine the sex of the animal and its size. There are a number of factors to consider when looking at tracks. After having nailed more than a couple of shoes on horses and trimming a number of hooves as a guide, horse trainer and riding instructor, I know that no two hooves are alike. Right and left, front and rear hooves each have different shapes. When you look at tracks, check the shape, size, travel pattern and how the imprints are placed in relation to each other. Look for drag marks and chips or abnormalities in the hoof. It is not a simple matter of size or shape that helps determine size and sex, it is a combination of factors. Don't fall into the trap of trying to categorize an animal only by the size of its tracks.

There are 30 different recognized subspecies of whitetail in North America. These subspecies differ in size and type of terrain they inhabit. Deer in swampy or soft soil have less wear on their hooves than deer in rocky terrain. The large subspecies of the north have larger hooves than the Florida Key deer, the Texas fantail or the small Coues deer. Like some humans, some big deer have big hooves and some have small hooves, so we have to speak in generalities. Usually older, bigger deer have bigger hooves than other deer in the area. This means that males often have the biggest hooves. One study shows that the width of the back of a mature buck's front hooves (when they are not greatly splayed) is wider than $2\frac{1}{4}$ inches (5.5 cm). Size is not enough to say that the tracks were left by a buck.

Obviously if you see drag marks from September on, in dirt or light snow, you can make a bet that the animal is a buck. Mature bucks walk stiff legged, and swing their toes out, which causes them to drag their hooves. In deep snow any animal may make drag marks. By determining the placement of the hooves, looking at the travel line, and the shape of the hooves, you can

Check the outline, depth, width and length of a print to determine whether it was made by a buck.

become certain. Because the buck carries a rack and has a swollen neck during the rut, it has a lot of weight on the front hooves. This weight is not carried directly over the hooves, however. The mechanics of this are similar to a fulcrum and lever, as when you use a long-handled jack to lift your vehicle. Because the added weight of the neck and rack are in front of the hooves they exert more pressure than the actual weight. This causes four different effects on the front hooves—they sink deep into the ground, the toes spread apart, the toes point outward, and the hooves drag.

There are three other factors to consider when you are looking at tracks. Because bucks make scrapes, especially dominant bucks, they round off the tips of their front hooves. Hoof prints that appear rounded on the tips are usually made by a scraping buck, meaning a breeding buck. This doesn't mean a trophy buck—a small-racked buck with a high testosterone level may be the dominant. Bucks generally travel in a straight, purposeful line. Bucks often step directly in or short of the prints of the front hoof with the hind hoof. Because does have a wider pelvis for fawning their hind hooves often land outside and ahead of the front tracks.

If you see one set of tracks in the fall, instead of two or three of different sizes, or if the one set of tracks lead to a scrape or rub it is probably a buck. Large clumped droppings nearby, or large pellets indicate a buck. A urine stream that points straight down, not a spray toward the back, is from a buck. By process of elimination, and following the tracks to read the other sign, you can make an informed guess on the size and sex of the animal, but not the size of the rack.

Droppings

When combined with other signs, deer droppings or scat can help you identify high-use areas. Droppings help determine size, sex, recent-use areas and type of forage eaten. The most noticeable indicators of droppings are the size and the freshness. Shiny or moist droppings are fresher than dull, dry ones. Shiny droppings often indicate recent use of the area, usually within the previous twelve hours.

The size of the droppings can indicate the size of the animal. Because of the different subspecies of deer, the size of droppings varies by locale. For northern whitetails, droppings less than ½ inch (1.25 cm) are generally those of does and fawns; droppings larger than ¾ inch (1.75 cm) are those of bucks. Bucks also leave clumps of droppings in cylindrical shapes—generally, the larger the diameter of the clump, the larger the deer. These clumps are often found in or near scrapes, rubs and buck bedding sites. To determine the length of the pellets I use my little finger. I know that the last joint of my finger is about 1 inch (2.5 cm) long; the fingernail is ½ inch (1.25 cm). The entire length of my little finger is 3 inches (7.25 cm), and I use it to determine the size of tracks. If you measure the size of the droppings, tracks and beds you find, you have a better idea of the size of the animals in the area.

Once you have determined the size and possibly the sex of the animals, you can determine when and where to find them. If you know the size and sex of the animals, you can tell which trails bucks use, and which trails does use. Prior to the rut, bucks often use different areas than does, and travel different routes than the does. Numerous droppings in beds indicates frequent use. Different size droppings and different size beds tell you that the area may be a doe/fawn area. Similar size droppings near beds indicate buck use, and possibly that the area is used as a buck bedroom.

Once a buck bedroom is located it is best to stay out of it, so you don't run the buck off. Keep the area in mind so you can hunt near it during the season after you establish the buck's direction of travel in the morning and evening. If you find lots of droppings scattered over a large area, it may be a feeding area. If you can determine what the animals are eating, it can tell you what time of year they use it. Many food sources are seasonal. There is no use spending time hunting in browse or a berry patch if the animals are grazing on agricultural crops or feeding on mast in a forest.

Beds

Deer bedding sites are often traditional, and used on a semi-regular basis. Daytime bedding sites are generally in heavy cover. Nighttime bedding sites may be in the open. Because does have their young with them, they require larger areas than solitary males, and they often use the same area, but different sites. Bucks often choose the densest or most remote areas, and use the same general sites. Bedding sites are often located on benches on the downwind side of hills.

Bedding sites vary both by time of year and time of day. Day bed areas are governed primarily by the need for security, then comfort. In warm weather, day beds may be in open cover with shade on high ground, often on north- or west-facing slopes where cooling breezes blow. They may also be in low-lying areas that remain cool. During

During warm weather, deer may be in places open to cooling winds, such as this low hill in a field.

cold weather day beds may be found on south facing slopes, where the animals take advantage of solar radiation when the sun is present. On windy days in cold weather, day beds may be in dense cover, low-lying areas, or on the downwind side of hills and slopes. Night bedding sites are not as traditional as day bedding sites, because their use is governed less by the need for security, and more by the availability of food and comfort. Deer often lay down near nighttime food sources. In warm weather, night beds are often found in open areas on hills, where breezes allow cooling and scent checking. In cold weather, night beds are often found in cover on the downwind side of hills.

Strong prevailing winds influence where and when game animals bed. Whitetails in many areas bed on the downwind side of hills and slopes. In mountainous regions, mule deer and elk often bed on the east side of slopes that protect them from strong winds. Many types of game choose the downwind side of hills, about a third of the way down from the top. Studies have shown that this portion of the slope has a "calm pocket" providing relief from the wind. This calm pocket also creates a swirling effect, where scents collect and provide animals with an advance early-warning system of danger from behind them. At the same time, the animals can hear and see any danger below. Being near the top also gives them an escape route.

The beds of northern bucks are usually longer than 45 inches (112 cm). Very large bucks may have beds up to 50 inches (125 cm). Doe beds are about 40 inches (100 cm), fawn beds 36 inches (90 cm) or less. Numerous beds of different sizes and ages indicate frequent use by females and young. Individual large beds in heavy cover indicate solitary males. A urine stream near the middle of the bed indicates a buck. Splattered urine near the back of the bed indicates a doe. Beds with nearby clumped droppings or large pellets, and rubs, indicate a buck bedding site.

Locating daytime doe beds tells you that you are in a doe-use area. There should be a nearby buck travel route with rubs and scrapes. Once you find doe beds you can either hunt the does, or follow the buck's trail to its core area to find the

Seven-year-old Tawnya points out a deer bed. During cold, wet or wind weather deer may seek shelter under evergreen trees.

buck. Find the does to find the bucks. Locating the buck's daytime core area is the purpose of following a rub and scrape route. Locating the buck's core area gives you the best chance of setting up near the area where it spends most of its time during the day.

Rubs

Rubs are one of the signs many deer species leave behind. Whitetails, elk, moose, mule deer and blacktails all make rubs during the rut. Rubs indicate areas the males use because of food, cover, water, a travel lane, or because females use the area. Rubs can tell you the social status, probable age, comparative antler size and how recently the area was used. The number of rubs in an area can tell you if you are in a high-use area. Numerous rubs in one location define a "dominance area" within the buck's home range. The type of habitat the rub is in tells you when the buck travels through the area, and if you are near its bedroom. If there are many small rubs, or in a heavily wooded area, you may be near the buck's bedroom. If there are rub clusters away from the bedroom you may be in a doe staging area. Rubs along a lightly used trail indicate that you are on a buck rub route in a travel corridor, which usually leads from the buck's core area to a nighttime food source, and from the food source back to the buck's core area. Rubs in the open are made primarily at night and are often near a food

source; rubs in cover may be made by the buck during the day and are often near buck or doe core areas, or in travel corridors. Old rubs indicate previous, often traditional, use areas. If the area hasn't been over-hunted, or the game run off, it should be investigated for recent use.

A whitetail rub is a visual and scent signpost left for other deer to help identify the maker. The bareness of the rub is easily seen, and the combination of scents is easily smelled by nearby animals. A whitetail rub route defines the buck's travel route during the rut. The amount of damage and the size of the tree help determine the stage of the rut and the relative size and configuration of the buck's rack.

A rub may involve two different actions: rubbing or thrashing the tree or other vegetation, and chewing or licking the rub. The rub is made when the buck rubs or thrashes trees and brush with the antlers and forehead for about 15 seconds, breaking smaller trees and brush or removing bark from the tree, and leaving forehead scent from the sudoriferous glands on the rub. The buck may then lick or chew the rub, leaving saliva and possibly nasal gland scent on the rub. Because the buck may have previously rub-urinated and then licked its own tarsal it may leave urine, testosterone and tarsal scent on the rub.

Elk and mule deer often rub in the same area year after year, but not on a regular basis, because they are wide ranging species and cover many miles during a day, and many more during the rut. Whitetails frequent a small home range in comparison to other species. A whitetail buck may use from 1 to 5 square miles (2.5 to 12.5 square km) during the rut. Because of this, whitetail bucks often rub in the same area, even use the same trees, and travel the same trails year after year. They often travel the route about the same time every few days during the pre-rut, before the does come into the breeding period. Once the does come into estrus the bucks begin to pursue them and may forget about following the rub route.

The rub route is a clear indication of where to find the buck on a semi-regular basis. It also shows where the buck beds, feeds and ends up at night in search of does. The rub route leads from the bedroom (where the buck often rubs on small saplings) often through several doe-use areas in succession, before ending up at a night food source. The buck may rub on his way back to the core area in the morning if he passes through wooded areas. If he travels primarily at night on his way back to his core area, he may feel secure traveling across open areas and therefore does not rub. I patterned a ten-point buck that had no rubs on the route back to his core area until he was well into the woods where he bedded. The side of the tree that the rub is on usually indicates the direction from which the buck came. Several rubs on the same side of trees along the route, and tracks pointing in the same direction, tell you which way the animal was traveling. A buck may have one or more rub routes leading to different food sources and doe core areas.

Bucks often have a cluster of rubs in a doe-use area or near a scrape in a "staging area" where deer gather near a food source. The food source may be in a wooded area, a meadow, or an agricultural crop. Staging areas are usually used in the evening, are often in cover near the food source, or in low-lying areas, where the deer remain concealed until about sunset.

The author examines a rub to determine which way the buck was traveling and how fresh it is.

Rub sites usually occur in areas containing numerous potential rub trees of the correct size. Most of these sites are traditional and show evidence of past use over several years. Traditional sites don't usually occur in areas that are too thick, or that don't contain trees of the correct rubbing size. Bucks in different areas rub on different types of trees. In Georgia bucks use shining sumac, black cherry, sweet gum, pine and eastern red cedar (juniper). Bucks in Minnesota use aspen, birch, cottonwood, sumac, cedar, pine, black cherry, red and white oak and willow. Many of these species have few lower limbs and smooth bark. Some of them, cedar and pine in particular are aromatic and are rubbed heavily. I have seen cedars, even with low-hanging branches, rubbed, and most of the lower branches broken or mangled. Depending on the type of trees in the area, the bucks often use their favorite species of tree. When they rub on small trees, bucks often use oak, willow, sumac, aspen, alder and cherry. One ten-point in my area uses pine, aspen and cedar. One big eight-point uses aspen, oak sapling (which he mangles) and alder. Knowing which trees a buck prefers may tell you which buck made the rub.

Many experts believe only big bucks rub on big trees. The problem is that the average hunter translates this statement to mean "trophy" bucks. Most rubs, especially those made early in the season, are made by dominant bucks 3½ years old or older with high testosterone levels. The high testosterone level helps make the buck dominant. Not all older bucks carry big racks. Some 3½-year-old bucks only have "respectable" eight-point racks that are not trophy class. Because of the young age of the bucks in an area, or the lack of other bucks, the dominant buck in an area may be a small-racked buck. I believe that rubs found on big trees are made by bucks with big racks. However, I have watched big-racked bucks use trees from 1 to 6 inches (2.5 to 15 cm) in diameter. Just because a rub is on a small tree it does not mean a small-racked buck made the rub. I have also watched a small-racked buck work a 9-inch (22 cm) tree. Most 3½-year-old bucks, with eight-point racks scoring in the 100 range, are able to rub 5- to 6-inch (12.5 to 15 cm) trees.

You may also be able to tell something about the configuration of the buck's rack by the rubs it leaves. Gouges on the right side of most of the trees indicate the buck may have a sticker or non-typical point on the right side. Individual bucks often rub at different heights on trees; a high- or non-typical rack may make it hard for a buck to rub except at one level. Gouge marks on trees adjacent to the rub may indicate a buck with long tines.

Types of Rubs

In their study on rubs and scrapes, Terry Kile and Larry Marchinton described three different types of whitetail rubs. The first rubs to appear (Type 1) are usually on small saplings 1 to 2 inches (2.5 to 5 cm) in diameter, and leave the trunk broken, but with little bark removal. These Type 1 rubs often start in early September, but decrease as the rut progresses, and their use often ends by early October. I find these rubs in open areas that are probably used at night.

These first rubs are replaced by Type 2 rubs, which don't leave the tree broken, but do have some bark removed, normally from only one side of the tree. During the study these Type 2 rubs were frequent in early September, less frequent in late September and early October, and peaked from late October to mid November. I find these rubs on 1- to 2-inch (2½ to 5 cm) trees in buck core areas, along rub routes, and near open feeding areas.

Type 2 rubs are followed by Type 3 rubs, which are longer and wider, with bark often removed from both the front and sides of the tree. During the study these highly visible rubs were present throughout the rut, and increased from September through late December. Because Type 3 rubs are visual, they are probably a signal to other deer in the area. I find these highly visible Type 3 rubs in semi-open areas along travel corridors and near staging areas and doe core areas.

I find another type of rub, similar to a Type 1 rub that is caused by a buck thrashing saplings or brush. The thrashing mutilates the brush or sapling, leaving it broken or mangled. I suspect that, because these thrashed rubs often occur in open areas, one or more bucks may use the area at

night. When you see saplings and brush that have been thrashed during the pre-primary breeding/scraping phase, or during the primary breeding phase, its a pretty good bet one or more dominant bucks are using the area.

Most deer hunters are familiar with traditional scrapes that bucks use year after year. It turns out that bucks also use traditional rubs. During their study on rubs, Woods, et al., found that bucks re-used some rubs during successive years, that bucks may reuse the same rub more than once a day, and that more than one buck will use the same traditional rub. The researchers defined a traditional rub as one that had been used for at least three years and was 3½ inches (8.5 cm) in diameter or larger.

They also found that 74 percent of the buck activities at scrapes occurred between 9 p.m. and 6 a.m. Only one mature buck was photographed near a rub during daylight hours. As to the time of the rut when the rubs were used, buck activity near traditional rubs in South Carolina began in August, rose in September, peaked during October,

The amount of mutilation on this rub indicates to the author that it is a traditional rub, used by one or more bucks in past years.

The bright coloration and appearance of the strips of bark on this rub indicate that it was recently made.

was lower in November, and was almost non-existent in December. This suggests that unlike traditional scrapes (which I found to be used most frequently during the two to three weeks prior to peak breeding during November in Minnesota) bucks use traditional rubs during peak breeding (which occurs in October in South Carolina).

During Woods' study the researchers found that four of nine bucks used one rub more than once. Individual bucks used the same rub from one to 33 days apart and one buck used the same rub three times in one year. They also found that bucks showed a preference as to which type of tree was used as a traditional rub; in South Carolina they used sassafras, Eastern red cedar and southern magnolia. In Minnesota I found that bucks often re-rub maple, pine cedar, aspen, birch,

cottonwood and white (burr) oak saplings. I often found traditional rubs on maple, aspen, birch and cottonwood that were at least 6 inches (15 cm) in diameter.

While all this information is interesting, it is only a bonus to discovering the travel route and core area of the buck. With the information gathered from walking a rub route, you should be able to set up along the route to ambush the buck. If you have time to observe the rub route and actually see the buck, you can determine the size of its rack, and what time the buck arrives at individual points along the route. If you don't see the buck during daylight hours, walk the rub route in the direction of the core area and hunt the buck in the evening. Get close to the bedding site on the buck's route back to the core area to hunt it in the morning.

The closer you are to the core area, the better your chances become to see the buck during daylight hours. Once the buck gets away from the core area it often travels under cover of darkness. Finding the buck's daytime core area is the key to hunting a rub route. It is where the buck is most likely to be moving during daylight hours.

T.R.'S KEYPOINTS

Rubbing and scraping signal the start of the rut. This may occur as early as late August or early September in the northern states and earlier in the southern states.

Most scent-marking activity (rubbing and scraping) occurs at night. Daytime rubbing and scraping occur mostly in the evening hours.

Nighttime scraping often occurs in semi-open and open areas. Rubs and scrapes in wooded sites indicate areas bucks may use during the day.

Rubs and scrapes are small dominance areas within a buck's home range. Scrapes near clusters of rubs may be used to attract does and bring them into estrus.

Bucks may make as many as 300 rubs per year, averaging 2½ rubs per day over a four-month period. During peak rubbing, bucks may make as many as 20 rubs per day.

Scrapes

Whitetail scrapes can tell you the social status of the buck, probable age, and comparative body size. If you understand scrapes they can tell you how recently and how frequently they are used. This tells you whether a scrape is a traditional scrape, which tells you if you are in a high-use or doe area. The type of habitat the scrape is in can tell you when the scrape is used. By reading rub routes and scrape lines and following them, you can locate the buck's core area.

The scrape is a combination sight and scent signal left for does, to help identify the social status, health, and the individual animal making the scrape. It is probably a signal to other bucks in the area that there is a dominant nearby. Other deer can see the mutilated overhanging branch, and the bareness of the ground and they easily smell the complex set of scents.

Scrape making by dominants involves two different signposts and four different actions. The usual sequence of scrape making begins with the buck rubbing a low-hanging branch over an open area with its antlers and forehead leaving forehead scent from the sudoriferous glands on the branch. It may rub near its eyes, possibly leaving scent from the preorbital gland. The buck then usually rubs the branch with its nose and mouth, and licks or pulls on the branch with its mouth. Because the buck may have previously rub-urinated, then licked its own tarsal it may leave urine, testosterone and tarsal scent on the branch. It may also leave scent from the nasal glands, and saliva, possibly leaving another scent. The buck then paws the ground with both hooves, using three to five strokes with first one hoof then the other, leaving interdigital scent on the torn up litter and dirt. The buck finally rub-urinates on his tarsal glands, leaving urine, testosterone and tarsal scent in the scrape.

The complex scent on overhanging branches and in scrapes is used by dominant bucks as a visual and scent priming source to bring does into estrus and synchronize breeding behavior between the sexes. It also tells subdominants that a dominant is using the area. Older dominant bucks make

Following rub routs and hunting active scrapes can lead to mature bucks like this one.

most of the scrapes, and begin scraping earlier than younger bucks. By attracting does earlier, the buck has a chance to breed more does.

In Marchinton's studies, scrapes were associated with game trails, old roads and small openings. These are all high-use areas that whitetails normally travel. Because scrapes are meant to attract does, frequently used or primary scrapes are often found near doe-use areas and buck dominance areas that may be evident by clusters of rubs.

Dominance areas are often found near staging areas downwind of food sources, and within individual doe-use areas. Staging areas are where deer gather (usually in the evening) before entering feeding areas they regularly frequent. This is especially true for does. If the buck is trying to attract does it is one of the best places to leave a signpost. Research suggests that a scrape in a doe-use area was probably made by a dominant buck. There should be a rub route nearby. If the rub route is near a trail, old road, stream or river bottom, the area is probably a travel route in a doe home range. If there is a nearby food source it may be in a staging area. If other signs confirm that the scrape is in a high use area, you should see deer on a regular basis, provided there is still nearby food and the area is not used at night.

Remember that most scrapes in open areas (like field and meadow edges), especially near doe-use areas, are used primarily at night.

The hoof marks in the scrape, direction of the scrape marks in the scrape, and where the dirt, snow or leaves are piled tell you the direction the buck was facing when it made the scrape. However, this will not tell you the direction the buck came from, because it may have to face a different direction to use a particular scrape. The direction of the rub route helps you determine which way the buck comes from.

In Georgia bucks use sweet gum, loblolly pines, greenbriar and dogwood to scrape under. Bucks in Minnesota use apple, plum, ash, elm, red and white oak, box elder, maple, pine and cedar. Many of these trees have few lower limbs, but often ones of suitable height. A twelve-point in my area uses red oak, mulberry, ash and pine. A big ten-point uses red oak almost exclusively. One eight-point prefers apple and plum. And so on.

Numerous scrapes in the same area can be caused by different circumstances. There may be more than one buck using the area, but using different trees. Bucks often scrape under the same tree, but not always in the same scrape, eventually creating what looks like one very large scrape. Several fresh scrapes together may only be the result of rutting urge, and they may never be used again. A dominant buck may make several small scrapes as a threat to lesser bucks, especially if the dominant is with a doe. Several frequently used scrapes indicate a high-use area—often a staging area, food source or travel lane.

Some experts feel that the size of the scrape determines the importance of the scrape. While this may be true, the recent use, frequency of use, and amount of mutilation of the overhanging branch are the best indicators of importance. Numerous bucks may check and even use the same scrape. Some of the bucks will rub-urinate and some won't while checking the scrape; but most of the bucks will thrash, lick and chew the branch leaving it mutilated. The mutilation of the branch may be a better indicator of the importance and frequency of use of a scrape, than the size of the scrape. I have seen big bucks make very small scrapes, use them frequently, and never enlarge them.

Most scrapes are made in the evening. If a scrape is in an open area it was probably made under cover of darkness; if it is made in an open area, near the edge of a field or ridge top, it may be at a staging area used in the late afternoon or evening. If it is made in an open area, near a nighttime food source, it may be where the buck feeds at night before returning to its core area in the morning. If the scrape is made in a heavily wooded area, it may have been used during daylight. Reading the signs of the rubs and scrapes tell you which way the buck leaves the core area in the evening, and which way it returns in the morning, and therefore the time when the scrape is visited.

The size of this scrape indicates that it has been used several times, and the fact that it has been pawed from different directions suggest it has been used by more than one buck.

Although deer "mouth-lick" branches at traditional scrapes all year long, bucks may not work these licking branches with their antlers until the velvet is removed. This may be as early as the first week of September in the northern states. Most of these early scrapes appear at or near open area food sources. They are used primarily at night, possibly infrequently.

Dominant bucks generally begin scraping earlier than younger bucks and make most of the scrapes. Scrapes prior to the breeding phase suggest a dominant buck, but not necessarily an older or large-antlered buck. Dominance is established by a combination of size, fighting ability, and most importantly testosterone level. A small-antlered buck with high testosterone levels may be dominant. The only reliable way to tell the size of the buck's rack is to see it.

Numerous bucks may visit the same scrape, but while bucks of all ages mark overhanging branches, they may not all paw the scrape. Scrapes with urine may indicate an older or dominant buck, particularly if the scrape is used during the two weeks prior to peak breeding. The amount of mutilation of the overhanging branch at a scrape may be a better indicator of the importance and frequency of use than the size of the scrape.

Scrapes in wooded or otherwise secure areas may be used during daylight hours. Bucks usually begin using these secure area scrapes more frequently as the breeding phase approaches. Some of these secure area scrapes are traditional and may be used several years in a row.

Traditional scrapes often occur within doe-use areas along travel lanes, in protected staging sites near food sources and near doe core areas. Traditional scrapes are often visited by more than one buck.

Types of Scrapes

Many experts claim there are three different types of scrapes; primary, secondary and boundary. Basically these designations define the importance and locality of the scrape. Primary scrapes are made in strategic locations with trails leading to them. These scrapes are often traditional (used year after year) because of the cover in the area.

They usually occur in staging or doe-use areas. Secondary scrapes are generally found in travel corridors, along trails, and in natural funnels between core and feeding areas. It could be said that all scrapes start out as secondary scrapes, but that some of them are elevated to primary status because of their importance, which results in some scrapes being used more frequently during the pre-primary breeding phase. Some scrapes are referred to as boundary scrapes because they appear along boundaries of a buck's home range, or between two different types of habitat. They are often located along trails, creeks, fences, old roads and field edges. Because of the openness of these areas these scrapes are often made at night. Boundary scrapes may be randomly made by traveling bucks.

For hunting purposes we can classify scrapes into four groups:

- Recently made scrapes.

- Infrequently used scrapes. I have seen bucks make four scrapes in an hour and then never use them again.

- Frequently used (certain times of a season), then abandoned scrapes. These scrapes are often near food sources that become depleted, causing the deer to seek other foods. If a more preferred food becomes temporarily available elsewhere, the deer may abandon a scrape but eventually return. All scrapes are abandoned at some time, either during or after the rut.

- Frequently used scrapes (most of the season). These scrapes are usually in doe-use or staging areas near food sources (corn, browse, and clover) that are used during most of the rut.

The recent use of the scrape, especially just before peak breeding, tells you the buck uses the area at that time. Any recent scrape is worth investigating further and possibly hunting. Recently used scrapes that are never used again, or are not used frequently, are not good hunting sites. Look for a higher-use area. You can only determine this by checking the scrape regularly or hunting it.

Frequently used scrapes, showing recent use, should be watched closely and hunted. Frequently used scrapes that do not show recent use should be noted because they may be traditional scrapes, used at specific times during the season. Try to figure out why the scrape was used and when, then use the information to hunt the area next year. Scrapes made early in the season may be made simply out of rutting urge. Scrapes made near early seasonal food sources may not be used after the food is gone and the does stop using it. This often occurs after the breeding period. If a scrape is near an all-season food source (browse, clover), and a more preferred food source (acorns, corn) becomes available, the deer may temporarily abandon the area and then return. A scrape in this area may be re-opened later.

Recently used scrapes made late in the season, after the breeding period, may be those of subdominants. They may begin scraping because the older bucks have quit checking their scrapes and exerting dominance. Frequently used scrapes of any type are often traditional, used year after year, used by subsequent bucks, used by numerous bucks, and possibly checked by all bucks in the area. Frequently used traditional scrapes in heavy cover may be used during the day and often occur in travel corridors and near doe use areas.

Determining how recently and how frequently the scrape is used helps you decide if you want to hunt near it. The importance of scrapes changes as the seasons change, as food sources are depleted or become available as the rut progresses. Scrapes may attract does, and may occur in traditional areas year after year, but they may be used only during certain times of the season. What you have to do is determine how frequently and recently they are used, and hunt them accordingly.

Scrape Age and Frequency of Use

The frequency of use and the age of scrapes determine their importance as a hunting site. To determine the frequency of use and age (recent) of the scrape examine it closely.

Reading Scrapes

R f	If there is still vegetation with fresh torn-up dirt, and it is not covered by leaves or snow, it has not been used frequently, but was made recently.
r+ f	If there is still vegetation with fresh torn-up vegetation or dirt, and it is covered by leaves or snow, it has not been used frequently, but may have been made recently.
r f	If there is still vegetation but torn-up dirt, and vegetation is dry or gone, it has not been used frequently or recently.
r f	If there is still vegetation but torn-up vegetation and dirt is dry or gone, or the scrape is covered by leaves or snow, it has not been used frequently or recently.
R F	If there is no vegetation with fresh dirt, and it is not covered by leaves or snow, it has been used frequently and recently.
r+ F	If there is no vegetation with fresh dirt, but it is covered by leaves or snow, it has been used frequently and may have been used recently.
r F	If there is no vegetation with dirt that is dry, or it is covered by leaves or snow, it has been used frequently but not recently.

In this chart, "r" stands for recent; "f" stands for frequency. The more capital letters and plus signs, the more attention the scrape deserves. Frequently used scrapes tell you where bucks often appear (usually traditional); recently used scrapes tell you where a buck has been lately.

CHAPTER 4

Scouting White-Tailed Deer

O nce you begin to understand white-tailed deer, you are prepared to choose a hunting area. Whether you are looking for property to buy, lease, rent or just use to hunt, get the best you can. The best areas provide for all the needs of the deer: security, escape and bedding cover (usually woods and rough terrain), food (browse in woods, grazing in meadows and agricultural crops) and water. If you are looking for trophy bucks, realize that they need abundant year-round food, minerals, a balanced population that is at or below carrying capacity for the habitat, limited hunting pressure and quality management so the bucks have a chance to live long enough to become a trophy.

Sooner or later, abundant food sources, with available water near security and bedding cover will attract game. If there is not enough food you can provide it through food plots and plantings. Minerals can be supplied year-round so the animals have adequate nutrients for growth, females have enough for developing young, and males have enough for antler production. A population at or below carrying capacity can be reached through selective hunting. Low hunting pressure can be achieved by limited access to private land, archery-only hunting, or terrain or habitat that other hunters don't want to hunt. Quality management of whitetails can be achieved by not taking any buck with less than a 15-inch (38 cm) spread.

Scouting is actually getting on the land to discover the high-use areas of the animals by the sign they leave behind. In order to scout properly you need to be able to interpret the signs. You should be looking for trails, tracks, droppings, beds, food sources, rubs, scrapes, doe home ranges, buck home ranges, staging areas, escape cover and areas used during inclement weather as protection.

Deer Hunting Land Criteria

Before choosing an area to hunt you should decide what your personal hunting criteria is.

- Are you just looking for an area to hunt?

- Are you looking for an area with high success rates?

- Are you looking for exclusive hunting rights to avoid other hunters?

- Are you looking to lease or buy land so you can practice habitat and game management?

- Are you looking for an area that has, or can produce, trophy animals?

Get a copy of the big game reports from the area. These reports can tell you the number of animals in the unit, the male-to-female ratio, the archery, gun and muzzleloader success rates, and the buck success. Some reports tell you which hunting period is most productive. Check the state record books, Boone & Crockett, and Pope & Young books for trophy success by county or unit, size of the animals, and year taken.

Asking farmers where they see deer as they work their land is a good way to find out about bucks on the property.

Once you have decided on your personal criteria, look for property that meets your needs. Personally, I want property I can control, where I can manage the habitat and the animals, and property that contains trophy animals or has the ability to produce them through management. I look for areas where trophies can be found. Because I live in southeast Minnesota I have an advantage. This area is the dividing line between three of the largest subspecies of whitetail, the *borealis*, *macrorous* and *dakotensis*. All of these subspecies produce trophy deer. The Boone & Crockett record book lists over 50 heads taken from this area. Any property here with good habitat has the ability to produce trophy bucks. I try to gain exclusive access to the land by agreement, helping out with some of the work, by rent or by lease.

While you are looking you should also be observing. Make note of where the males and females feed, where the food sources are, where their home ranges are, and where you think they travel during the hunting season. Bucks often use the same core areas during the fall, but travel through as many doe home ranges as they can each night during the rut. If you know where the females are you know where the males are likely to travel during the breeding season. Find out how much of the property you can get access to, and how many other hunters are hunting it. Decide if it is worth it to hunt just a small area of the home range, or whether you should look for another area to hunt.

Trophy Areas

Whitetail trophy areas have certain factors in common. Many of them occur along hardwood river bottoms and creek drainages with adjacent agricultural land. This combination provides numerous edges between woods and stream, stream and meadow, woods and meadow, woods and field, and field and wetlands. These edges provide numerous plant species the animals can choose from at different times of the year.

The farmland/forest mix provides excellent food. Farmland provides varied agricultural crops; the forest provides browse, acorns, nuts, seeds and fruits. These two habitats attract and concentrate

does and consequently big bucks. These river bottom or creek drainages provide dense and rugged habitat for bedding, escape and security cover, and often limit hunting pressure.

If you can, find an area that contains all the animals' requirements. Being able to hunt the farmland, woods, and transition zones gives you the option of hunting the preferred food source areas of the deer at the right time. If you have access only to farmland, you lose the opportunity to hunt woods when the acorns drop, and to hunt the security and bedding sites where the animals spend most of their time. My personal preference is private land adjoining public lands where the game is heavily hunted and escapes to the less hunted private land. If I have to hunt small properties, I prefer wooded areas that offer security, bedding, and food sources near heavily hunted public lands. This gives me the opportunity to hunt the edges of the woods near trails coming and going to food sources.

You can find out where trophy animals are by using an information network to help locate them. Talk to the taxidermists, archery and gun shop owners, mail carriers, delivery-truck drivers, road crews and other hunters in the area, anyone who might see or know where trophy animals are. If you hear of a good area, find out who owns the property, if you can hunt it, and under what terms you can hunt. Long-range scout the property first by driving around it looking for animals.

Public Land or Private Land

Hunting public land can be frustrating because other hunters may hunt the same area you do and ruin your perfectly planned hunt. If you have to hunt public land, try to hunt at a time when, and a place where, there are few hunters. Get as far away or as deep into heavy cover and rough terrain as you can. Hunt the archery or muzzleloader season. Hunt weekdays when other hunters are working. One of the best strategies is to thoroughly scout, observe, record and pattern the animals before the season, then get in early and get your animal before it gets smart and other hunters overrun the area. Studies show that most animals are taken within the first two days of the season.

If you can lease land, try to secure most of the home range of several animals, so that you are the only one hunting them. Larger properties give you the opportunity to improve the habitat and use management practices to selectively cull the animals. To properly manage a herd, a large area is needed. Dominant males commonly travel several miles during the breeding season and property lines mean nothing to them.

Another advantage of private land is that you can control hunting pressure by limiting hunter numbers. Too many hunters on a property can drive the animals out, make them wary and hard to hunt. Once you have located the core areas they should be designated as refuges and not hunted except as a last resort. This ensures the animals will not be disturbed in their resting areas, so they will stay on the property.

The combination of good habitat, controlled hunting and providing refuge for the animals not only holds them in the area, it also attracts them. By using good management practices to keep the herd within the carrying capacity of the habitat and taking only larger bucks you will begin to see more trophies.

Locating Deer

There are four different techniques to systematically locate animals: scouting, observing, recording (keeping a journal and marking on a map) and patterning (learning deer movement to predict the best place and time to hunt). Once you have chosen an area to hunt you should scout, observe and pattern the deer if possible to determine how many there are, where they travel, what time they travel and how big the bucks are. This information should be recorded in a notebook along with the current weather conditions. Note the locations of food sources, home ranges, core areas, bedding sites, staging areas, escape and security cover, trails, rubs, rub routes and scrapes. This information helps you decide if you want to hunt this particular property or look for another one.

Obtain a topographical map and an aerial photo of the area so you know where the woods, fields, roads, water, saddles, gullies, hills and valleys are. Mark their locations on the map or photo. Then begin the actual process of locating the animals. Use a combination of scouting the property to locate sign for high-use areas and observing the animals from vantage points to prove what you find. Just because you see sign in an area doesn't mean the game use it at a time when they can be hunted. You can pattern the animals while you watch the area to see when and where they are most active.

Brush or small trees that are mangled in what is referred to as a "rage rub" may indicate the presence of two or more dominant bucks in the area.

The object of scouting, observing, recording and patterning deer is to pinpoint the home range of the does and bucks, their core areas, the day and night bedding sites, the security cover used to get away from hunters and out of inclement weather, the food sources, the staging areas, and the trails. To be successful as a hunter you need to know the property as well as the animal. You need to know where to find the animals under any and all conditions. The only way to do that is to put in some time and effort scouting, observing, patterning and recording the animals' activity.

Scouting can tell you the areas the animals use, and whether they use it during the day or night. The only way to be sure what time they use a particular area is by observing and recording the time and place where you see them. Once you have scouted, observed and recorded their activity you can begin to pattern the animals.

You can pattern female groups and individual males. By patterning the females, their home range, core areas, staging areas, food sources, and the times they use each one, you can locate the males once the rut begins. Or you can pattern an individual male, which can be one of the most difficult, time-consuming, satisfying and successful ways to hunt. Patterning is often considered a hunting technique, but it should be considered as a part of locating, because it is a valuable asset in finding game, and it makes hunting much easier.

Become a Predator

One of the reasons humans aren't successful when they hunt is because they don't become a hunter. Putting on hunting clothes and picking up a hunting weapon does not make you a hunter. Taking a weapon into the field with the intention of hunting does not make you a hunter. It does not make you what you should be if you want to be good as a hunter—what your ancestors were—which is a predator.

The difference between a hunter and a predator is that the predator has an intimate knowledge of the game in the area, the area itself, and knows where to find the game at the current time of year, time of day and under the current environmental conditions. If you have hunted the same property for several years you understand what I mean.

The more experience you have on a particular property, the more familiar you are with it. The more experience you have hunting, the better your hunting skills and hunting techniques will be. The more experience you have hunting a particular species, the more you will know how it reacts at particular times of the year, and times of the day, under different environmental conditions. The more experience you have hunting a particular species on a particular property, the better you will be at predicting where to find the animals on that property under all conditions. To be successful as a predator you have to know the land, know the species, know how the species will react under all environmental conditions, have experience hunting the species, use proven, successful hunting techniques, and be a good hunter.

One of the biggest problems for hunters is not knowing the lay of the land. Hunters don't know the land because they may not have hunted it before, or have not spent enough time and effort scouting it. No one can teach you the land. You have to learn it yourself, and the more hours and years you spend on it, the more you will know about it. You can cut corners by getting information from someone who knows it, and by having and being able to use topographical maps and aerial photos. Maps and photos will give you an idea where the preferred habitat of the game is. But if you don't understand the game, you won't know what type of habitat it prefers, and where to find it under all environmental conditions.

You can learn about the game by reading, listening to others, watching videos and observing the game itself. The more time and effort you put into trying to understand the game, the better you will be at predicting where, and when to find it. The best way to learn about the game is to research it thoroughly to gain all the knowledge you can about it, then spend time and effort watching and hunting the game yourself. Knowledge is only a partial substitute for personal experience.

Rub routes, like this one in a low-lying area, are often used within an hour of sundown or sunset.

You can learn hunting techniques, but without good hunting skills (learned through personal experience) even the best hunting techniques won't do you any good. Hunting skills (being quiet, unseen, unscented and a proficient shot) must be sharpened by putting them into practice over several years. The traits of patience, perseverance, persistence and curiosity are possessed by predators, and can be taught through self-discipline. These traits and skills must be combined to make a good predatory hunter.

Knowing you should stay downwind of big game, knowing when to sit still and be quiet, knowing that if you hunt all day you're chances of seeing game are good, and doing it is not the same thing. Knowing there may be an animal just over the next hill, and going to find out are two different things. Knowing that sitting it out in cold, windy, wet weather will probably help your chances of seeing a trophy whitetail, and suffering through the weather are two different things. Knowing that putting in more time and effort will help you

learn more, see more and become a better hunter, and not doing it are two different things. Reading and listening can help you know and understand the game, but you have to make the time, supply the effort and build the experience if you want to become a predatory hunter.

Scouting

You can scout any time of the year, but it's especially important during the hunting season. Game activity changes as summer passes into fall and fall passes into winter. Available food sources, falling leaves, weather, hunting pressure, the rut and shorter days all affect game movement, and unless you scout all season long you will not be able to reliably predict when and where to find the animals.

Post-Season Scouting

Once the deer is in the freezer and the hunting equipment is put away many deer hunters lose interest in going to the woods. But for the dedicated deer hunter the next hunting season is just beginning. After the hunting season the weather may turn cold, the winds may blow strong and the snow may deepen. Walking through deer habitat at this time of the year may no longer be an adventure, it may be more of a chore. But for adventurous deer addicts who want to learn more about deer and deer habits, this is a great time to be in the woods.

Scouting to learn the lay of the land, and to learn the "high-use" deer areas of the area, is one of the keys to connecting on big bucks.

Deer tracks that were obscured in the dirt and leaves of fall may now be easily seen in muddy or snow-covered trails. What looked like matted-down grass in the fall may now prove to be a buck route, the drag marks of the buck's front hooves showing clearly in the snow. Following trails in the snow can eventually lead you to bedding areas, showing you where the big buck you couldn't find hid during the hunting season. When you don't see the buck again next year you'll have a good idea where to find him. Trails can show you food sources the deer used during those inclement days when you sat on your stand without seeing anything. They can also show you escape routes you didn't know were there.

One of the best ways to locate the bucks you couldn't find during the hunting season, is to observe feeding areas and scout for field sign after the rut or the hunting season is over. If you have rain or snow in your area, get out the door when the rain or snow lets up and backtrack the buck trails until you find their core areas and bedding sites. If you do this while the bucks are on their fall home ranges you'll know where to find them next year during the hunting season. If the bucks in your area move to winter ranges, and if you can't or don't do it until after the bucks have moved, you can still use the information to watch the deer through the winter and into the spring.

Following buck trails along rub routes while bucks are still on their fall home ranges helps you pattern them well before the season. And, while the bucks may not use the exact same trails as they do during the rubbing and scraping period, they will probably use the same gullies, roads and bottlenecks that offered them protection all year long. Once you know the bucks' general routes, it is much easier to locate, pattern and hunt them next year.

While scrapes are difficult to detect under the snow, the bareness of the rubs are still evident on the trees. Following a buck trail from rub to rub is quite easy in the snow and you may find some scrapes. If whitetails have a long breeding season in your area, some of the bucks may begin scraping again 20 to 30 days after the primary breeding period as the younger does come into estrus for the first time and older does that were not bred the first time experience a second estrus. In areas with low buck numbers, where a lot of does don't get bred, there may be a third breeding period with more rubbing and scraping.

If you are really addicted you can watch the deer to learn their travel routes and the times they use them. I start out watching deer by picking one or two sites where I can see as much habitat as possible. I like to choose a stand that overlooks a food source, open area or bottleneck to watch deer. A tree stand overlooking a food source is an excellent spot. Any location that lets you see a long way, like a hill that overlooks bedding areas and travel lanes, is good. I do this a lot during

The author examines a leafy area that has been pawed by the deer, to determine what the deer are eating at that time of the year.

the pre-rut to pattern the bucks, but I also do it in the winter because it cuts down on the amount of time I have to scout and observe in the fall before the hunt. It doesn't take me long to figure out where to set up after I see a buck two or three times while I am scouting.

The more time and effort you spend scouting, observing and patterning deer after the hunting season, the less time you have to spend doing it before the next season. If you shed hunt, winter scouting to locate rub routes and buck bedding areas is an excellent way to stumble across a shed antler.

Spring Scouting

While many hunters begin to pattern a buck in the fall when it starts to shed velvet and make fresh rubs, it is actually easier to pattern a buck in the spring. Although the lesser-used buck trails

Pre-Rut/Rubbing Phase: Deer shift from summer foods to available mast, fruit and agricultural crops and browse more. Locate food sources as areas to hunt.

Dispersal Phase/Fall Home Range Shift: Buck bachelor groups begin to break up and bucks become more aggressive. Bucks may move to new core areas where they can bed by themselves. Find fresh rubs in secure areas to locate buck core areas. All deer may move from summer home ranges to fall home ranges. Find the areas where the does have moved.

Pre-Primary Breeding/Peak Scraping Phase: Bucks begin to travel rub routes, making scrapes two to three weeks before the primary breeding phase. Locate buck rub routes and groups of scrapes. As the rut approaches bucks shift from their own travel routes to those used by the does. Locate both buck rub routes and doe trails for areas to hunt.

Shorter Daylight Hours, Colder Temperatures and Falling Leaves: Deer move deeper into cover as leaves fall. Move hunting sites deeper into woods or to current travel routes. With less daylight and fewer leaves deer shift their activity times from daylight hours to dusk, dawn and nighttime hours, and from covered daytime trails to more open night trails. Scout to find areas deer use during daylight.

Primary Breeding Phase: As unbred does come into estrus the bucks abandon rub routes to chase does. Spend all day on rub routes near buck and doe core areas or doe-use areas with scrapes. Bucks begin to use open trails at night. Locate daytime use areas or bedding sites to hunt. Doe groups begin traveling together. Be aware that there may be many deer in the area.

Rest Phase: Bucks may return to their core areas and feed heavily. Hunt buck core areas and travel routes leading to and from food sources.

Post-Primary Breeding Phase: Bucks begin to travel together. More than one buck may appear—wait for the big one. Bucks begin to travel with the does. Locate doe feeding areas to locate bucks.

Pre-Late Breeding and Late Breeding Phases: Bucks begin chasing does before and during the late breeding phase. Hunt near buck bedrooms, rub routes, and doe-use areas.

Post-Rut: Bucks may again return to their core areas. Hunt in or near the core areas.

Winter Home Range Shift: Deer may migrate to winter ranges. Locate buck core areas/winter ranges to hunt.

may not be as visible in the spring, the rubs and scrapes are clearly evident. Even if the buck that initially made the rubs and scrapes has been shot, other bucks will often use the same rub route. The trails used by bucks are chosen because they offer security. They are usually the safest means of travel from the buck's bedding area through adjacent doe-use areas to nighttime food sources. Remember that in the fall the buck isn't just going from his bedding area to food sources, he is traveling through all the adjacent doe-use areas that he can cover in a night. If you are looking for buck trails remember that they often parallel the more heavily used doe trails, intersecting them only at bottlenecks or near scraping and bedding areas. If the trail shows little use it may be a buck trail. Look for buck sign: large tracks, drag marks, rubs or large clumped droppings. Buck trails, especially rub routes, may be traveled by only one buck, once a day, in one direction, and show very little evidence of being used. If you find vague trails lower or higher on ridges than doe trails, or trails that run through heavy cover, follow creek bottoms, sloughs or forested lake shores they may be buck trails.

If you find doe-use areas in the spring you will probably find rubs and old scrapes. Once you find the doe-use areas, or a feeding source, and the rub route, it is a matter of backtracking the rub line of the buck to find its bedding area. If you want to be sure of the buck's bedding area, now is a good time to go into it, even though you may spook the buck. By the time hunting season rolls around the buck will have forgotten about your intrusion and will begin using his preferred bedding area on a regular basis again. If you don't see a deer in the area, check for beds, large droppings or piles of clumped droppings over 1½ inches (3.8 cm) in diameter. Although does may make clumps, I usually see them in buck bedding areas and in, or near, scrapes. If there are a lot of droppings in one area with rubs on adjacent trees it is a good bet you have found the buck's bedroom.

If you haven't found the buck's rub line, the buck bedding area is a good place to look for it. With the use of a topographical map or aerial photo to show you where the food sources, roads and bottlenecks are located, you can make a good guess which way the buck travels and where he will end up. You can usually find the buck's trail out of the bedroom and follow it by the rubs. If it's possible and you have access to all the property the buck uses, follow the entire route from the bedroom to the food sources and back to the bedroom again. Bucks may leave little evidence of their passing on the way back to their bedding area in the morning. I think they are often in a hurry to get back and don't take much time to mark their trail until the peak of the rut.

You can usually find their trail by the tracks and rubs left from previous years. Once you know the buck's rub route you know where to find him, but unless you have seen him regularly, not when to see him. When you have found the trails, doe use areas, buck bedding areas and rub lines, record their location on a map.

If you see deer record the time, place, weather conditions, food sources, activity and other factors in a journal so you know where to find the deer in the fall. With the information gathered in the spring it takes less time and effort to locate, observe, record and pattern the deer before the hunt.

Pre-Season Scouting

Summer is a great time to start getting ready for the deer-hunting season. It's a great time to begin looking from the roads for bucks in velvet. If it is a cool day, it's a good time to look for deer trails, tracks, droppings, beds, and old rubs and scrapes that may help you figure out where the deer were last year during the hunting season, and where they hopefully will be this year.

It usually takes time, patience, work and know-how to connect on trophy-class bucks like this one.

When you are getting ready for the deer season you should begin watching for deer at likely food sources in late summer. In the upper Midwest I usually begin looking for deer during late July and early August when I often see does and fawns feeding. I get pretty serious about locating bucks during the last two weeks of August and the first two weeks of September, when I often see bucks traveling together and sparring in preparation for the rut. Does, fawns and bucks will be loading up on succulent grasses, clovers, ripening grains, berries and sedges in late summer. Don't expect to regularly see the bucks using the same food sources as the does, because bucks often stay closer to their bedding areas than does. If the bucks do use the same food sources as the does, they often show up later than the does.

By scanning with a good set of binoculars as you cruise roads near agricultural crops and meadows during the morning and evening, you can find out which fields the bucks are using. If you are there early enough in the evening you may see the bucks arrive and be able to determine where they came from. If you stay late enough you may be able to see them go to either another food source or back toward the bedding area. Because bucks don't travel very far at this time of year, their bedding area should be within about ½ mile (0.8 km), and probably closer to ¼ mile (0.4 km). When you see bucks at early morning food sources, stay there long enough to see which way they leave. In the morning the deer usually work their way slowly from open areas, and finally into heavy brush or woods, where they feed and bed intermittently throughout the day. Once you know the route the deer take back to their core areas you can set up along it during the hunting season.

A buck's rub route leaving its core in the evening usually winds through several doe-use areas before ending up at a nighttime food source. Then it often leads through other doe-use areas as the buck moves back toward its core area in the early morning before daylight. You should be able to find several rubs along the evening rub route, and scrapes in the transition zones near food sources, along field edges, and near doe core areas.

Following the buck's rub route back to its core area in the morning can be difficult, because bucks often travel under the cover of darkness in early morning, as it allows them to feel secure enough to travel in the open. Since the bucks are traveling in more open areas during the night, there are very few trees, which means you may not find any rubs or scrapes along the route the buck uses on the way back to its core in the morning, until the route goes back into a wooded area. I think part of the reason that bucks don't make rubs and scrapes along the trail back into their core areas is because they are in a hurry to get back, and they don't take much time to mark their trail until the peak of the rut. But, you can usually find their trails by their tracks, and the rubs left from previous years.

If you have time to observe the rub route trails you can learn where and what time the buck uses them. Finding the rub route and knowing when the buck uses it helps you choose the right time and place to hunt. If you don't have time to watch the trail you can use a timing device to let you know what time the buck comes through the area. Of course, this won't tell you the size of the buck's rack. If you want to know the size of the rack without being there, you can use a camera to take the animal's picture as it passes by.

If you use a timing device be sure to get one with multiple timing functions, so that you can tell you how many deer came through the area. If you get one of the new cameras that are connected to a timing device, the camera can tell you the sex of the deer, and the size of its rack. If you don't use a timer to find out the buck's travel time, the best strategy is to find its core area and set up as near to it as you possibly can, using different stand sites for morning and evening hunts, and for varying wind conditions. By getting close enough to the buck's core area to watch it, but far enough away from the core area that you don't alert the buck to your presence, you increase the chances of seeing the buck during daylight hours.

Hunters often say that during the hunting season they can't find the big bucks they saw while they were scouting from late August to mid September.

During September you may only have a few days to connect on a buck like this, because it may move from a summer home range to a fall home range sometime between mid September and mid October.

That's because the bucks probably weren't in the same area. Once the bucks shed their velvet, they start to become more aggressive. Eventually they won't put up with each other. While some of the bucks may stay in the same area, many of them move to new core areas where they won't come in contact with other bucks.

Some of the bucks may move out of their summer home range to go to their fall home range, which may be as little as ½ mile (0.8 km) to as far as several miles (km) away. This dispersal and fall home range shift usually occurs within two to three weeks of when the older bucks begin to shed velvet. In the upper Midwest it generally occurs sometime between the first and last week of September. By mid October the bucks have usually moved to their fall home ranges. If you plan on hunting after October 15, you may have to start scouting all over again, because the bucks you saw and hunted from late August to mid October may have moved to their fall home ranges.

Since bucks usually start making new rubs and scrapes in the areas they use in the fall, the best way to locate them is to look for fresh rubs and scrapes. When you find fresh rubs and scrapes in areas where they may not have previously occurred that year, set up where you can watch that area, to see which bucks are there. Once you find the buck you want, you can backtrack its rub route to locate its core area, where you can set up to take the buck.

Familiarizing the Deer

You can't scout all season long without alerting the animals to your presence. But you can reduce their alarm by scouting at the right time and getting them accustomed to you. Familiarizing is getting the animals used to you, the sight and sound of you walking, and the scent you leave behind. By scouting as much as possible during the daytime in areas the animals use (but not while you are scouting), they become familiar with you.

Don't act like a predator while you scout, walk purposely from place to place, checking food sources, night bedding sites, trails, rubs and scrapes.

Don't sneak through the woods as if you were hunting because you will alert the animals. Erratic searching, or moving hurriedly from place to place in a wandering manner is predatory behavior and alarms the animals. Act like you are out for a stroll, with very little stopping, and avoid areas that you know the animals are currently using. I scout open feeding areas from 10 a.m. to noon when deer are in brush or wooded areas. I scout wooded feeding areas from noon to 2 p.m., but I stay away from known core areas. At this time most of the deer will bedding in their daytime core areas and won't move much. I do spook some animals, but if I continue out of the area they soon return to normal behavior.

I have taken this technique to such an extreme that I actually walk down the trails and rub routes of the bucks to get them accustomed to my scent. My smell dissipates enough by the time the animals use the trails that it doesn't alarm them. I wear rubber knee-high boots from La Crosse, rubber gloves and a Contain or Eliminator scent reduction suit while I scout, and I use Scent Killer or Scent Shield to eliminate human odor. I still leave some scent behind, and the first time the animals come across it they become alarmed. But, as long as they don't hear me or see me (because I am not there) they soon get used to the smell. I have used this method to put out mineral with my bare hands and found animals eating it within two hours. Familiarizing works to get animals accustomed to your smell. Then, when hunting season comes around and the animals smell you, they are far less wary than they normally would be. Usually they are only curious.

Observing, Recording and Patterning

Observing deer on a regular basis should be an important part of hunting and locating deer. Observing is watching the animals regularly to learn their daily habits, reactions and patterns. Observing should be done from vantage points where much of the property can be seen without interfering with the animals, and from areas where the animals aren't aware they are being watched. You can watch from stands and blinds overlooking agricultural fields, trails, runways, gullies, valleys, lakeshores, etc. Use as many vantage points as it takes to watch most of the property. Especially watch the areas that are hard to see, where the game travels. The more area you watch, the more you know about the activity of the game.

Observing takes time and effort, but not as much as you would think. After watching the property for a few weeks you should be able to predict where the animals move and at what time. The more time you spend observing before or during the hunting season, the better you will be able to predict where and when to find the animals under similar conditions later on.

Recording can be the most useful technique in hunting. Make notes in a journal regarding the date, temperature, wind-chill, wind speed and direction, barometric pressure, lunar conditions, time of day, light conditions, amount of foliage, available food sources, breeding phase, game numbers, sex, and direction of travel. On an aerial photo, topographical map, or map of your own making, mark where the escape cover, food sources, home ranges and core areas, trails, rubs, and scrapes are. When you know where

When you see a trophy-class buck like this one, be sure to make notes of the time and place you saw it and the weather conditions at the time.

animals were in the past, you can predict when and where to find them on any given day. Animals in different areas have preferred times and conditions in which they move to open food sources. In inclement weather they have preferred use areas depending on the current weather conditions and food availability. By a combination of scouting, observing and recording you can learn where to find the animals under any and all conditions, and at what time of the day. By recording deer sightings you begin to see daily activity times and routes, which help you pattern both the does and the bucks. Once you know where the buck's bedroom is, and have marked the rubs and scrapes on your map, you should be able to determine the buck's rub route and begin to pattern the buck. You should also know the daily travels of the does.

Patterning deer is determining which trails the animals use in their daily travel on a regular basis, and at what time. You can pattern female groups, but more often males are patterned. Patterning is done by using a map and marking the core areas of the deer in the area, the preferred food sources, and the trails they use regularly to and from these areas. If you find numerous rubs, mark them on a map, and know which trail the bucks use by observing them. Then, if you note the time the buck arrives at certain points along its travel route you have an idea of where to set up for it during the hunting season.

The ideal way to pattern a buck is to know where it is bedded during the day, what time it usually leaves the core area, the route it usually takes, when it arrives at the first place you can hunt it, when it arrives at the first staging area, when it arrives at each doe-use area, and where it makes rubs and scrapes. You should also know the route it takes on the way back to the core area. Once you have all this information you can choose several hunting sites along the rub route to be prepared for changing weather and travel times.

Knowing where the core area is, and what time the animal usually leaves and returns to it is crucial to successfully pattern a buck. Bucks spend the most continuous amount of time during the day in their core area, so the most predictable place to find a buck is in the core area. The time when the buck leaves the core area in the evening is often the most predictable time of its daily movement. Being near the core area in the evening when the buck leaves before sundown may be the only chance you get on a nocturnal buck. If the buck finds an estrus doe, encounters danger, stops to feed, or just takes his time, he may be late along the rest of his route.

Bucks often return to their core area before daylight, but if they find a doe at night or early in the morning they may be late going back to the core area. This happens most often during the peak of the rut when the buck is chasing does. The time when the buck returns to its core area during peak rut is totally unpredictable. The buck may stay with a doe for up to three days and not return to its core area, bedding near the doe instead, or it may return to its core area at any hour of the day. The period when the buck is most predictable, using its rub route at regular times each day, is during the scraping phase, before breeding begins. Once breeding has begun, does start coming into estrus and buck activity is less predictable.

I begin scouting, familiarizing, observing, recording and patterning as soon as I gain access to the property. The only time I don't do full-scale scouting is if I gain access to the property less than two weeks before I intend to hunt. By scouting too close to the hunting period, without previously familiarizing the animals, you alert them, and you may run them out of the area. If I can't scout, I rely on observing and recording to pattern the animals.

Locating the deer needs to be an ongoing process because as the season progresses the habits, routes and times the animals travel will change. If you don't watch them for the entire season you will not be able to predict their movements. After a few seasons of keeping a journal you will be confident of knowing where and when to find the animals, not only in your area, but also in most areas, under most conditions.

CHAPTER 5

Avoiding Detection

When game animals see a sight, hear a sound, or smell a scent that may come from one of their own kind, or a predator, they want to identify it. Their reaction is to become alert, be ready to evade danger, and try to identify the source. If the source can't be identified, and there are no other clues through sight, smell or sound the animal may freeze, flee or investigate. If the source is identified as possibly being dangerous the animal may either freeze or flee.

While you are hunting you want to think like a predator but you do not want to look, smell or act like a predator. Animals use their sense of smell, their sight and their hearing to detect the sight, scent or sound of a predator, and to alert them of danger. Hunters are detected by game because they give off scents associated with a predator, and scents that are unnatural to the environment. Humans make sounds associated with a predator or are unnatural to the environment. They move and gain the animal's attention, stand in the familiar upright form of the human predator, or appear as a large blob of color that stands out from the surroundings. If you want to be successful as a hunter you need to avoid detection through the sights, scents and sounds you produce.

Avoiding Detection by Sight

The survival of an animal depends on its ability to detect danger. Any sudden, jerky, continuous or unnatural movement is noticed by most game animals. A single game animal is constantly alert for danger, looking around before entering openings, raising its head while feeding, and looking for movement. Animals in groups, herds or flocks often have at least one animal on alert all the time. The more animals in the group, the more animals there are to share time watching, and the more time each individual animal has to eat and rest. It is often the older females that are alert; the younger animals have not learned the importance of watching yet.

The upright, moving form of a human is unlike any other form, except that of a standing bear, which is also a predator. When an upright form appears as a solid dark blob it only helps to make it more visible. Even if game animals have not seen a human or a bear, an upright moving dark form alerts and often alarms them. Most animals have seen and been hunted by humans, and have learned to avoid and fear them. To avoid looking like a predator or a hunter you need to camouflage or conceal yourself and stay still.

Conceal yourself from detection by staying in natural cover and shadows, or using a pit, blind, or tree stand. Simply being above big game, whether uphill or in a stand, places you out of the normal range of vision of the animal.

Once you are in a concealed place, keep movement to a minimum and avoid any sudden or continuous movement. When you have to move, do it while the animal isn't looking, or when it can't see you and move as slowly as you can. When you are hunting animals that travel in groups, be aware there may be some animals you don't see. To avoid being seen while you are hunting or going to your hunting area, try to avoid going through open areas, and use natural cover, terrain and shadows. Choose hunting sites that are out of the animal's line of sight—off to the side of game trails, in gullies, behind natural cover, or use a tree stand. Use portable ground seats or stands where there is ground cover, and portable blinds where there is no available cover.

Camouflage can be a substitute for concealment, but concealment is no reason not to use camouflage. What if you decide to leave your place of concealment because the weather changes or you don't see any animals, and you are caught in the open when you see game? What if you see game on the way to your hunting area, before you are concealed? I always wear camouflage that either matches the color and surroundings where I hunt or breaks up my outline, whether I am firearm or bow hunting, taking pictures or scouting. I don't want the animals to know I am there if I can help it.

Dr. Greg Bambenek, better known as "Dr. Juice" used his knowledge of deer behavior and deer scents to take this buck.

Camouflage

Camouflage is used to make objects resemble the surroundings by using a similar pattern or color or to break up the outline of the object so that it is unrecognizable. The best way to break up the outline of a large object is by using large areas of contrasting colors. The larger the object is, the larger the camouflage needs to be to effectively break up its outline. A pattern that works well on hunting clothing is usually too small for a hunting blind. The farther you get from a camouflage pattern the more it begins to merge into a solid color. For camouflage patterns to work effectively on large objects, or at distances, they need to be big.

Contrasting colors help break up camouflage patterns by giving the illusion of depth or a difference in distance. When used correctly, light colors appear either as being in front of or behind darker colors. When used in large patterns, light colors often appear as light or sky showing behind the darker portions of the camouflage, which makes the design appear as if there were objects at different distances.

Many hunters have accepted the promotions of camouflage designers who claim one pattern will work anywhere. This may be possible with a generic pattern, but a bark pattern does not work in tan corn or cattails anymore than a tan corn or cattail pattern works in a green woods. The simple fact of the matter is no one camouflage will work in all situations. If you intend to hunt in a variety of different surroundings, or hunt wide open country, choose a camouflage with a large pattern of contrasting colors. If you hunt only one type of habitat choose a pattern and color to match the habitat at the time of year you hunt it.

When you are hunting on the ground in woods, wear a camouflage that looks like bark, leaves, branches and twigs. If you are hunting from a tree stand use a big, open pattern with a light gray background. Look into your tree stand sometime from a deer's point of view and you will see a lot of sky. If you want to disguise yourself you should not wear a solid bark pattern; it will make you look like a big gray or brown blob hanging in a tree. You should wear a branch, twig or leaf pattern

on a gray sky background that resembles what the animal sees from its point of view. If you hunt in fences, cornfields, cattails or alfalfa, wear a corn, grass or cattail pattern. If you hunt in an evergreen forest wear a large green pattern. If you hunt in rocks, sagebrush or desert, use an open pattern that blends in with the surroundings.

If you are hunting early in the archery season when the leaves are green, wear green camouflage. Woodland green works well in green hardwoods and evergreen forests. When the leaves turn brown, your camouflage should change. Universal brown with its tan background works well in many brown surroundings. Once the leaves have fallen you should switch to a more open pattern, with gray that resembles the sky, or tan that resembles dead leaves on the ground. If you hunt when there is snow on the ground your pattern should be even more open, with a white background, whether you hunt in a tree or on the ground.

Deer Vision

There has been a lot of controversy about how and what deer see. Scientists believe many hoofed animals see the colors blue and yellow. Because these colors are not natural in many environments, you should not wear them. But blue and yellow combined make green, which is present in the gray and brown of nature. Wear browns and grays. Deer are red/green color blind, but they do see colors in the ultraviolet range. Many of the earliest camouflages used dyes with ultraviolet brighteners to print the fabric. These dyes were used primarily in the gray colors. With the research that Dr. Jay Neitz has done, there is little question that deer and other hoofed animals have the ability to see the light reflected from those early dyes.

Ultraviolet brighteners and dyes have the same effect as a white shirt washed in commercial detergent with brighteners, even in low light conditions when most of us hunt. When it is seen under an ultraviolet light, it shines. If you are wearing a camouflage that uses dyes with ultraviolet brighteners it will shine. When you are stationary in a tree stand a deer may not see you, or it may dismiss any shine it sees because it is

Deer are most active in semi-open and open areas within a couple hours of both sunrise and sunset.

accustomed to bright objects in the sky. But if you move you may be spotted. This is especially true in low light conditions at dawn and dusk. If you doubt that big game animals see better in the dark than humans, and that they see ultraviolet light, ask yourself if you could run through the forest at the speeds the animals do at night, without running into a tree or tripping. Deer species see better in low light conditions than humans!

If you own camouflage containing UV brighteners you don't have to stop wearing it and buy new clothing. Products like UV Killer, available from Sno-Seal, can be sprayed on your clothing to effectively stop ultraviolet reflection and prohibit game from spotting it. A bottle of spray is inexpensive, will treat your entire wardrobe, and your clothes can be washed up to five times before they need to be retreated. The minimal cost is well worth it if it helps you go undetected. If you are in doubt about your clothing check it under a UV light to see if it shines. When you buy clothing look for the UV Free hangtag, or ask if the clothing contains UV dyes before purchasing it. Most camouflage manufacturers now insist that UV-free dyes are used to print their patterns, but it doesn't hurt to check.

In many states the use of fluorescent orange is mandatory for firearm hunters. Most of these states require a minimum of 400 square inches (2560 sq cm), worn above the waist that can be seen from all sides. Some states also require that a hat or a hatband of orange be worn. Some states allow orange camouflage as long as 50 percent of each square foot (900 sq cm) is orange. The orange color required by hunters cannot be made without UV dyes. This leaves the hunter very visible to the game. With this in mind, and because I often hunt private property where safety is not as much of a factor as on public land, I wear as little orange as I can while still being safe. Instead of wearing solid orange I wear orange camouflage where allowed, and treat any orange clothing with UV Killer. Studies have proven that UV Killer stops ultraviolet reflection, but actually makes the orange more visible to the human eye.

Concealment

Concealment is using natural, manmade or portable blinds: trees, rocks, gullies, ridges and other terrain, shadows, or elevated stands to hide or stay out of the natural line of sight of whatever you are trying to avoid. If there is available concealment that will not alert animals of your presence, and it does not significantly alter your ability to see, move, hunt or shoot, you should take advantage of it. Take any legal advantage you can get.

Tree stands are the preferred means of whitetail hunting by many hunters. Permanent stands are the most comfortable, but confine you to one spot. Unless you have numerous stands in productive areas you limit your hunting options. Portable tree stands give you the option of moving to high-use areas as the situation dictates. Choose a stand that is easy to set up, lightweight, compact, noiseless, comfortable, and strong enough to support you and your gear. The more portable, compact and lightweight the stand is, the more likely you are to use it and move it, which is how it is meant to be used, and should be the reason you haul it around. If you are content to sit in one spot all year, choose a large ladder stand with a swivel seat, or construct a permanent enclosed blind. But don't expect to be as productive as the mobile hunter who moves his stand every two to three days.

If you hunt in areas where there is little cover, you can build a blind of nearby materials, or put out a portable hunting blind. Natural blinds should be made from available nearby materials. They may be as complex as a four-sided pile of brush, branches or rocks with the addition of blind material to one or more sides, or as simple as a bush, tree stump, gully, ditch or fallen log. A portable blind should be put out well ahead of the season to familiarize the animals with it. It should

If you hunt in open areas make sure you are either well camouflaged, or that your hunting site keeps you out of the direct line of sight of the deer.

be roomy enough to be comfortable, lightweight and compact enough to be transported, easy to set up or assemble, with a camouflage that matches the habitat you intend to use it in. I have field-tested a number of different blinds and find that most of them work for gun hunters, but many do not offer enough room for archery hunters.

The ground stand is one of the most overlooked, highly productive means of avoiding detection for hunters for a number of reasons:

- Game animals easily recognize the upright human form.

- Hunters don't realize that camouflage should have a large pattern of contrasting colors to break up their outline.

- Hunters wear ineffective small patterns that blob up at short distances.

- Deer have learned to look up into trees and identify dark camouflage-clad forms as sources of danger.

During my studies I had access to 13 tree stands, all of which would have been productive for a rifle hunter, most of which would have been productive for a shotgun, muzzleloader or handgun hunter, and many of which would have been productive for the archery or crossbow hunter. However, there were times while I was hunting a dominant buck and none of the useable tree stands were in range. There were times when I realized that I was spending too much time in one area, so I moved to another area where I had never set up before and stood or sat on the ground. I had deer feed within 5 yards (4.5 m) of my position in the open.

Many hunters don't use this method because they don't feel confident of avoiding detection on the ground, and many hunters don't feel comfortable standing or sitting on a rock, log or at the base of a tree. The confidence factor will come after you have used this technique a few times and have seen the positive results. The comfort factor is easily addressed by taking along a folding campstool. You can improve a campstool by adding shoulder straps and a storage bag to it. With this simple stool you can set up anywhere you find game, move quickly when the wind or weather dictate, and avoid detection by being on the ground and presenting a low profile (that does not resemble the upright human form). The comfort and safety of this hunting method will also help you stay longer and become more productive. A folding stool is one of the most lightweight, portable and compact hunting tools available to hunters.

Avoiding Detection by Scent

Scent gives away many hunters, and they never realize it. Most hunters are careful to wear camouflage, go to their stand in the dark or when the animals are not expected to be near it, and be quiet when they approach their hunting sites and while they hunt. Because they don't see game at these times some hunters believe they have gone undetected. However, they may have

To avoid deer smelling you as you lay a scent trail on the ground, use a stick held out to the side of you rather than behind you, and use a cover scent on your boots.

been smelled by the game, either from the scent they left behind, or from the scent they gave off at the stand. Any big game animal that smells a human or another unnatural scent in its home range will become wary or avoid the area where it made contact with the scent. Scent left behind by hunters has caused many deer and elk to avoid the area or to become nocturnal.

To be successful as a big game hunter you must take precautions so the game will not detect you by the scent you give off or leave behind. I have seen hunters place their clothes in a plastic bag to protect them from contamination, take them out of the bag once they get to camp, put them on, and then wear them while eating and sitting around the campfire—collecting cigarette and wood smoke, bacon grease, spices, alcohol and other odors. I have also watched in amazement as hunters wear their boots when they stop to eat at the local restaurant and gas station. Wearing the same boots they intend to hunt in, they get out of their vehicle, step onto the gas- and oil-covered concrete, and fill up the gas tank, sometimes spilling gas on their hands, clothes and boots. Next they go into the restaurant, filled with its wonderful odors that cling to their clothes and boots, order a meal, and head for the rest room, where they step in Lysol- or detergent-washed floors, urine and cigarette butts. All those smells travel with the hunters to the field where they will be immediately discovered by even the dumbest yearling.

Body and Clothing Preparation

There are several ways to keep from being scented by game: avoid, eliminate, suppress, cover up, and block. You can avoid being smelled by staying downwind of the animal. This is not always possible, especially when the wind swirls or the thermals change, so you must take other precautions. You can eliminate the source of some human odors by using antibacterial/deodorizing body soaps such as Scent Killer or Scent Shield. To eliminate odors on your clothes wash them in unscented detergents designed specifically for hunters. After you have eliminated the source of most human scent from your body and clothing, you can suppress more of the remaining odors that build up while you walk to your hunting area or at your hunting site by using body and clothes sprays.

You can also cover up any human or unnatural odors with another stronger, natural scent. Many companies offer earth, sage, pine and cow urine cover scent. Each of these scents should be used in areas where they would naturally occur. Use pine scent in areas where pines occur, but not in oak woods or agricultural areas where there are no pines. Products that can be worn in almost every situation are earth scents and cow urine. Most animals are familiar with cow urine, often in conjunction with human odor, and smelling the two scents together does not alarm them. I have used this product successfully for elk and deer in the Rockies, and for deer in the wilderness, agricultural and even the urban areas of Minnesota.

There are other products that can help you reduce or eliminate human scent, but they need to cover the areas of your body where these odors are likely to come from. These areas include your head and hair, your nose, your mouth, any facial hair, your neck, your armpits, hands, groin, buttocks, and feet. While scientific research has shown that activated carbon suits are ineffective at reducing or eliminating human perspiration odors, and it also appears that there is no way for the average hunter to reactivate or desorb these suits as the manufacturer claims, there are some other products that look promising. Contain clothing uses anti-bacterial agents to reduce bacterial odors associated with human perspiration. According to the manufacturer, the antibacterial agent is good for the life of the garment and washing will not diminish its effectiveness. No Trace and Eliminator use cyclodextrin, the same active ingredient as a popular air freshener, to trap odors, which, according to the manufacturer, can be released from the suit by washing it in cold water without detergent.

Hunters often forget two areas that transmit a lot of human and other odors--their hands and feet. Very seldom do I see hunters, including my own clients, wearing gloves as they walk through the

Drippers with buck or doe urine are a good way to attract bucks to your stand location.

woods while they push branches, grass and weeds out of their way. Every time they touch an object they leave scent behind, and that scent that can be detected by the game. I always wash my hands thoroughly, spray them with an odor killer, and put on gloves before I hunt. If I intend to put out scent or hang a dripper, put out a decoy or make a mock rub or scrape, I wear rubber gloves so I don't contaminate the area. When I remove my gloves for shooting I take the odor killer out of my jacket or day pack and re-spray my hands, clothing, the inside and outside of my hat and my boots.

Most hunters take the precaution of wearing rubber-bottom boots to eliminate odors but they don't realize that the boots themselves may produce odors. New rubber gives off an unnatural odor that can alert deer, elk and other game. Before wearing new boots they should be cured in the sun for two weeks to eliminate the odor. If you wear leather boots, or boots with leather uppers and waterproof them, the scent can be detected. Deer and elk will spook at the scent of mink oil and other products. I use Sno Seal beeswax to waterproof and preserve leather because it is a naturally occurring substance that does not alarm game animals. I also use silicone on my boots and clothing, and have never seen an adverse reaction to silicone if it is applied a few days before hunting. I use all-rubber knee-high boots if the weather is nice. When it gets cold I switch to LaCrosse pack boots treated with Sno Seal and Silicone Water Sealer. When I wear nylon upper boots (such as those by Danner) I treat them with the same products. To help eliminate any foot odor I sprinkle baking soda in the boots on a regular basis and wear Odor Eaters with polypropylene socks to wick away any moisture. I also spray my boots on both the top and bottom with an odor-killing spray before hunting.

While conducting a mock scrape study, Dr. Ben Koerth used human urine as the only scent in some of his mock scrapes. His game cameras recorded bucks using these mock scrapes, and urinating in them. His research showed that buck visits to mock scrapes dosed with human urine were "not statistically different" from those on which he used buck urine. Koerth told me that the mock scrapes with human urine attracted more deer than the mock scrapes with doe scent, and stated, "There is no indication that human urine scared deer at all."

Overkill

There is no question that the way I prepare myself for a hunt is overkill, but it works. I saw 469 deer in 74 days one year (many of them under 20 yards/18 m), so I believe in my system. and am not about to change how I prepare to hunt. In this case I live by the motto, "If it ain't broke, don't fix it." Whether I am hunting elk and mule deer in the Rockies or whitetails and bear in the Midwest I prepare my clothes and my body the same way. I wash my clothes in odorless detergent that does not contain UV brighteners then hang them outside to dry. I never put my camouflage clothing in the dryer. The revolving action of the dryer is abrasive and wears down the outer layer of the fabric causing the colors to fade, and the camouflage to be less effective.

After the clothes dry I put them in a plastic bag or directly into my waterproof duffel bag. In the bag I place some of the vegetation from the area I am hunting. When I am in the Rockies I put in pine needles and aspen leaves. When I am hunting in the Midwest I use acorns and oak, maple and other leaves. I always have dirt in the bag. If I hunt out of state the first thing I do when I get to camp is put local dirt in the bag. I don't care if the clothes are dirty as long as they don't smell of human or unnatural odors, and they do smell like the surroundings. The bag, with my clothes and boots, is kept outside, where it is not likely to pick up unwanted odors. Once I get to camp I hang the clothes outside to air out, and pick up the local smells. I don't air them out near the fire or kitchen.

The day of the hunt I get up early, eat a bland breakfast (usually cereal and milk but sometimes toast and peanut butter), then take my shower. If I have eaten bacon, eggs, pancakes and syrup, or eggs with ketchup, I wash off any lingering odors. I use an antibacterial, odorless hunter's soap, making sure my hair, armpits and groin are clean. I also brush my teeth with baking soda. Then I spray my skin with an odor killer, put on my underwear and spray it, using liberal amounts of the odor killer on my armpits and groin.

I dress in clean, non-hunting clothing, climb into my previously gassed up truck and drive to my hunting spot. Only when I am at the hunting area do I open my duffel bag, take my hunting clothes out of the sealed bag I keep them in, take off my traveling clothes, and put on my hunting clothes. Next I put on my camouflage and boots, which by this time smell like the local vegetation and dirt, and spray my clothes with odor-killing spray, making sure I cover the tops and bottoms of my boots, my gloves, and the inside and outside of my hat. Only then am I ready to step into the woods.

While I am walking to my hunting site I step in any puddles or mud along the way, and brush up against the vegetation to get more of the local smell on my clothes. Just to be sure, I pour cow urine on my boots. Then I walk to my site, staying off the trails unless I have previously familiarized the animals to my scent. Once I get to my stand, I spray my neck, face and hands with odor killer again, then spray a cover scent on my clothes, and place a couple of felt pads with cover scent upwind to mask anything I might have missed. It's a lot of work, but I can honestly say that to the best of my knowledge I was not scented all year by any deer when I took these precautions, even with deer 5 yards (4.5 m) downwind.

Avoiding Detection by Sound

When human beings hunt they produce sounds associated with predatory behavior and sounds that are unnatural to the surroundings. Both types of sounds alert the game. Any noise that resembles predatory sounds like loud, halting walking, extremely quiet, stealthy walking, breaking twigs, branches swinging or snapping back, dirt, sand, snow and gravel grating, and splashing water, will alert game, even if it comes from one of their own species. Sounds that are unnatural to the environment include fabric rustling, fabric dragging on vegetation, shoes or boots hitting the ground, squeaks, clicks and scraping of metal, coughing, spitting, nose blowing, voices of humans, vehicle noises, leather creaking and numerous other sounds. Unlike humans, animals are acutely aware of every sound around them. They must be aware of these sounds to avoid danger and possible harm.

To avoid the game detecting you by predatory or unnatural sounds you can eliminate, suppress

One way you can avoid bucks from spooking as you walk through the woods is by walking with the wind.

or disguise the sounds. You can eliminate many non-movement sounds by simply being aware of the sounds that alert game and not making them. Sitting still and moving slowly eliminates many movement sounds. When you have to move, do it when and where you are unlikely to be heard– when the wind blows or the leaves rustle. Use available terrain and vegetation to suppress sound. Wear quiet clothing and boots. Brushed cotton, saddlecloth, fleece, and wool are all quiet fabrics. Leather and rubber can be quieter than nylon upper boots.

You can suppress the sound of walking by placing your feet carefully, avoiding vegetation, and by slowing down and walking softly. You can disguise the sound of walking by imitating the tempo of the game in the area. I found myself doing this recently without knowing it. I was hunting elk in Michigan and I heard an unfamiliar sound. But, when I stopped to listen, I didn't hear it. In the back of my mind I knew there was some unnatural sound. When I started walking again I realized I was making the sound. I had heard deer all morning, the fast "tch, tch, tch, tch" sound of deer on leaves. But I was making a slower "tssch, tssch, tssch" sound, like an elk. I probably picked it up while guiding for elk all those years in New Mexico.

Because archery hunters spend a lot of time at stand sites, these areas should be cleaned of any debris and limbs that may brush against clothing, or get in the way of shooting. Archery hunters are usually careful about clearing shooting lanes, removing branches around their shooting site, and removing rocks, leaves and twigs from ground blinds. Gun hunters are often not as careful because they don't need to get as close to the animal, but all hunters should practice cleaning the hunting area. Clean up permanent stand sites well before the hunt. If time permits I clear my stands a month or more in advance, so the animals become accustomed to the change in the habitat. While I am doing this I clear the trails I use to go to and leave my stand. That way, there is less chance of making noise. I also make a point of going to my stand at least an hour before I expect the game, so that the area has a chance of settling down.

CHAPTER 6

Attracting Deer

The best way to attract deer, especially older bucks, is to deceive them by using a combination of the sight, scents and sounds of a deer. Once you have located the appropriate high-use area by scouting, observing, patterning and recording you can use scent and sound to attract the deer from long range. Calls and rattling may bring in deer from as far as ½ mile (0.8 km) away. Scents may bring deer in from several hundred yards (meters), especially if a scent trail is left. Once the deer have been attracted to your position, they may hang up because they detect you, or they hear and smell a deer, but don't see one. Decoys add a security factor for the deer. They can bring deer in close, and can position them for a shot. By using a combination of sight, scent and sound techniques, you can convince the deer there are real deer near you, and attract them to your position.

When you are using food, scents, calls, rattling or decoys to attract animals there are two things to remember. First, the best way to get an animal to come to you is by being in a place it is used to, comfortable with and already going to. It's much easier to get the animal to come to you if it routinely uses the area. If you are not in a regularly used area, then the animal should feel secure in the area, which should provide concealment or nearby escape cover. If neither one of these apply then you should be in a travel lane, or near one in a feeding area the animal is going to. Why should the deer come to you if it knows what it wants is in another location? Second, using the best hunting techniques won't help if you produce a sight, scent or sound that alarms the animals, or alerts them of your presence. Be careful to take precautions to avoid detection and go completely unnoticed when you hunt.

Using Scents

Scents are one of the most widely used methods of attracting deer. Manufacturers have responded to demand by providing a wide range of products in different forms: sprays, liquids, gels and solids. There are buck, buck-in-rut, doe, and doe-in-estrus urine scents, forehead, tarsal, metatarsal and interdigital scents, food, curiosity and secret formula scents. Many hunters use fox, coyote, mink, raccoon and skunk scents, as either cover or curiosity lures. Others use unnatural or human scents to block deer from using escape trails. This vast array of scents can be confusing if you don't know which scents to use, or when to use them.

Deer scents fall into different categories based on how they are used and how deer respond to them. These categories are: recognition/trailing, sex, territorial/dominance, food, curiosity and blocking. Recognition/trailing scents are present all year long and can be used all year. Sex scents are most prominent during the rut and can be used during any part of it. Territorial and dominance scents are most prevalent during the rut and should be used then to be most effective. Food, curiosity and blocker scents can be used all year long. Many of these scents fall into more than one category and can be used for different purposes. They can all be used effectively to hunt deer, if used properly and at the right time.

Deer pheromones, the scents given off by deer, are used as a means of communication. Pheromones serve to stimulate a behavioral response in another animal. Whitetail pheromones are present in the forehead, interdigital, tarsal and metatarsal glands, while estrogen and testosterone are found in the urine. There may also be pheromones associated with the nasal, pre-orbital, preputial and salivary glands. Many of these scents are used in combination during rub-urination, rubbing and scraping, and are interpreted by individual sexes and age classes differently. When used by themselves, these scents may be interpreted differently than when they are used in combination with another scent or scents.

Because recognition and trailing scents are present all year they can be used any time during the rut, or any time of the year, without fear of alarming deer. However, forehead scent is most prevalent during the rut and is more effective at that time. Because deer are curious about their home range and often exert dominance (even does) in their core area, they investigate any new scent to find out which deer is leaving it.

High amounts of testosterone in urine signals a buck's sexual readiness to does. Estrogen in the urine of a doe signals sexual readiness to bucks. Both buck testosterone and doe estrogen levels rise during the rut. Bucks readily respond to estrus urine, or doe-in-heat scents, soon after they shed their velvet through the second and possibly the third estrus, which may occur in January, even in northern latitudes. Because bucks are curious, estrogen can be used anytime of the year to attract them.

Does move a lot when they are in heat, sometimes traveling outside their core areas, possibly in search of healthy dominant bucks to breed with. It has been suggested that does can determine the physical health of the buck by the amount of protein in its urine. The doe may choose the buck it breeds with by the combination of the protein, testosterone and tarsal from rub-urination. Testosterone scents may attract does to a particular area, in turn attracting bucks because the does are there. Bucks may respond to testosterone out of curiosity, dominance or territoriality.

Urine-based scents are used because it is thought that bucks determine if a doe is ready to breed through the Flehmen sniff, which introduces urine to the vomeronasal organ. But the vomeronasal organ accesses a part of the brain that regulates reproductive physiology, and does not elicit the immediate response needed to ensure successful breeding. In contrast, the nose accesses parts of the brain associated with immediate behavioral

responses. So using urine may not be the way to go about attracting a buck. It has been suggested by several researchers that bucks detect pheromones through stimulation of the nose (rather than the vomeronasal organ), and that the stimulation of the nose is what elicits approach and copulation by the buck. Urine may not need to be present for a buck to detect an estrus doe. The buck is probably able to determine the readiness of a doe by the chemicals in vaginal secretions. If this is true, the best way to attract a buck is by using the vaginal secretions of a doe in estrus, not urine or urine-based scents.

Both the signposts of rubs and scrapes are dominance areas of mature bucks. These signposts signify areas used by the buck. The rub route is the path the buck travels as it goes through an area. The area along the rub route and the nearby areas are often traveled by the buck during the rut. Each rub on the route contains scents from the forehead glands of the buck. In addition, bucks often lick their rubs, and because they sometimes lick their own tarsal after rub-urinating there may be urine, testosterone, tarsal and saliva on the rub. This combination of scents is a territorial sign proclaiming dominance by mature bucks.

These same scents may also occur on the overhanging branch at a scrape (forehead, urine, tarsal, testosterone, saliva, possibly pre-orbital) because the buck sniffs, licks, chews and rubs

As this buck's hormonal levels rise it will shed its velvet and become more interested in the scent signals given off by other deer, especially does.

This buck is checking out the scent in a Wildlife Research Center dripper.

the branch with its forehead and antlers. Urine, testosterone and tarsal are also deposited in the scrape during rub-urination. The buck also leaves interdigital scent on the trail of its rub route and in the scrape as it paws the ground. This combination of scents is again a dominance and territorial signal to other bucks, and the sign of a mature dominant, breeding buck to does.

The complex combination of scents left on signposts occurs primarily during the rut. The scents of the rub occur as soon as bucks begin to shed their velvet. The scents of the scrapes begin shortly after rubbing begins, but become most evident from one to two months later. These scents can be used anytime once the rubbing phase occurs to attract bucks, but they become less effective after the primary breeding phase. Because a dominant buck makes rubs and scrapes as a prelude to breeding (to express dominance) it is impelled to check out the smell of any unknown buck intruding on the area, therefore these scents work especially well during the pre-primary breeding/scraping phase.

Food scents can be used anytime and anywhere. Because these scents do not contain pheromones, they usually do not alarm deer. The deer in my area of southern Minnesota eat corn, apples, acorns, squash, grapes, vegetable greens and many other hard-to-find foods that I leave out in the winter, spring, summer and fall. They also take advantage of foods in areas where they don't normally occur. Whitetails, mule deer and elk readily eat apples in the mountains where few apples occur. Once they are accustomed to finding these foods in an area, you can attract them by using similar scents, even if baiting is not allowed.

Because deer need to be familiar with their home range, they want to know about anything new. Many of the responses of deer to pheromones, urine, sex and food scents can be attributed to curiosity. In that respect all these scents attract deer out of curiosity. Deer have been known to investigate WD 40, gun oil, mink oil and several secret formula deer scents. Deer, elk and moose will investigate urine and pheromone scents of fox, coyote, raccoon, skunk and other animals, as long as the concentration is not so high as to alarm them. While most of these scents are used as cover scents to avoid detection, they can also be used to attract deer. I once watched a doe trail me by the fox scent I had on my boots. She followed along about ten minutes behind, just like a dog with its nose to the ground.

Some hunters use blocking scents to move deer to their position. While this is not actually attracting deer, it is a means of getting deer to come to you by blocking all trails but the one you choose. By strategically placing human scent, predatory scents from dogs, coyote or wolf, or large amounts of metatarsal scents associated with alarm on the trails you don't want deer to use, you can direct them to you. Blocking works especially well in areas with numerous parallel trails near core areas, or in heavy cover. You can also keep deer from using normal escape routes and avoiding you, by blocking the trails you don't want them to use. Blocking scents can be used anytime of the year and can be used effectively during any phase of the rut. If you are hunting a food source with numerous trails leading to it, block some of the trail several yards from the food source to force the deer to use the trail where your stand is placed. Try using a smelly pair of socks.

T.R.'S KEYPOINTS

Wary bucks responding to rattling or calls generally approach from downwind. Use buck-in-rut, tarsal, forehead, doe urine or estrus scents to add realism and bring bucks into range after being attracted by rattling and calls.

Using scents, like rattling and calling, works best when security factors are high. Deer prefer to move during low light conditions, when there are low wind speeds, and when few hunters are out.

Scent added to a buck or doe decoy provides the final stimulus to bring in reluctant bucks and distract their attention from your position.

Where to Use Scents

Most hunters use scents to attract bucks. Remember that adult bucks responding to scent invariably try to get downwind to check the scent and to detect danger. Also remember that adult bucks try to remain in cover. You can set up in the cover if you are sure the buck won't detect you. Try to position yourself crosswind of the buck's travel route to avoid detection. If there is nearby cover the buck will use, and a more open area crosswind of the cover, set up in the open area. Give the buck the cover while you wait in the area it won't use, and where you won't be detected. You can also set up downwind of the buck's approach while luring the buck to a position upwind of you. If you are archery hunting, be sure to place the scent close enough for a shot. If you have to set up upwind of the buck's approach, take extreme precautions to avoid detection. Don't put your stand in a direct line with the buck's line of travel as you may be seen. For the same reason you should keep your stand site a comfortable distance from the trail itself, far enough away to avoid detection, but close enough for a shot.

When you are using scent to attract bucks during the pre-rut/rubbing phase get as close to buck bedrooms and feeding areas as you can, or set up along the travel routes between the two. During the pre-breeding/scraping phase you can set up near rubs or scrapes along wooded rub routes. Prior to the primary breeding phase these areas are traveled regularly and you should be able to pattern the buck along its rub route. During the primary breeding phase, when the bucks may be with estrus does, bucks are unpredictable, but they may still frequent rub routes, doe use areas, and feeding areas. During the rest phase, the bucks often return to their core areas and nearby feeding areas. Three to four weeks after the peak of the primary breeding phase, you can expect a late breeding phase, when the bucks begin traveling their rub routes again. They can be found near their bedrooms, and with does in staging and feeding areas, where you should set up. During the post-rut the bucks again return to their core areas and seek high quality food sources to put on weight for the winter. Set up near buck bedding and feeding areas during this time.

The author hangs a dripper near his tree stand to attract one of the trophy-class bucks that use the trail leading to the cornfield below.

When and How to Use Scents

The type and amount of scents (pheromones and hormones) that deer produce and that other deer react to, changes as the rut progresses. Knowing which scents are most prevalent, and which scents the deer are most likely to respond to during the different phases of the rut can help you attract deer.

During the pre-rut, bucks often engage in sparring matches to establish dominance. They also feed heavily to put on enough fat to get them through the rut. They search out succulent fall greens such as clover, new cut hay, alfalfa, grasses that remain green, ripening berries, mast crops like acorns and beechnuts, and ripening agricultural crops such as corn, beans, and vegetables. If food sources are sparse bucks may respond to food scents, especially if acorn production is poor.

Bucks respond to any of the recognition/trailing, sex, territorial/dominance, and curiosity scents at this time. Because they have not begun using their rub routes the broadcast method of scent dispersal is most productive. Once you have chosen a high-use area to hunt, and a place to put your stand, decide where to place the scent. It can be hung from trees on felt pads, film canisters, drippers or other dispensers.

When I archery hunt, I place the scent crosswind or upwind of my position, about 15 yards (13 m) from my stand and 15 yards (13 m) apart, and wait for the buck to come by. I hang up one or two felt pads with doe or doe-in-estrus scent, but I don't leave scent out when I'm not there. If a buck comes to doe scent and doesn't find a doe he probably won't fall for it again. By taking the scent out every day you don't educate the buck.

For gun hunting during the rut, five to ten dispensers can be placed in a straight line or arc, upwind or crosswind from the stand site to attract wide ranging deer. The dispensers should be placed 20 to 30 yards (18 to 27 m) apart to spread the scent over a wide area.

During the scraping phase bucks regularly travel their rub routes and visit dominance areas of rubs and scrapes, and doe-use, feeding and staging areas. When I am hunting a previously

patterned buck during the scraping phase near a rub or scrape, I am fairly confident of the trail the animal uses and I don't need numerous dispensers. Because I have patterned the buck and am hunting before the breeding period, I am fairly sure the buck will come by me sometime within a week, unless he meets an estrus doe first or is spooked by another hunter. I am basically using the scent to position the buck for a clear shot. By using scent I also have a chance to bring in any lesser bucks in the area. If I am hunting in an area I have not hunted in before, I prefer to hunt during the evenings, because most scenting activity occurs at that time. If I find a rub route, I backtrack it until I think I am near the core area and set up as close as I can without alarming the buck. Otherwise I look for staging areas near food sources the does use in the evening.

Because bucks may still be feeding at this time of the year, but they are beginning to proclaim dominance and look for estrus does, food, territorial/dominance, recognition/trailing, curiosity and sex scents may all work. You can use the broadcast method of scent dispersal in

Within a couple hours of sunset or sunrise, dominant-class bucks are most likely to check drippers along rub routes or near scrapes in semi-open areas like this one.

wooded areas and travel lanes, make a mock scrape or mock rub route, or hunt near existing rub routes and scrape lines, especially those in wooded areas leading to food sources.

To get bucks in close, make a mock scrape and a mock rub near one of the buck's rubs or scrapes. Drip a line of interdigital or tarsal scent across the trail the buck uses and lead it to the mock rub. Remove the bark from the tree with a wood rasp, then drip forehead scent on the rub. Wear rubber gloves and boots while doing this so you don't contaminate the area. The mock rub should be placed in a shooting lane near your stand where the buck will stop to investigate, often sniffing the mock rub.

I make a mock scrape under an overhanging branch with the heel of my boot, rattling racks or a stick. I pour forehead scent on the branch and plenty of tarsal in the scrape. Then I hang an Ultimate Scrape Dripper with doe-in-heat or buck urine over the scrape, or near my stand in a shooting lane. This combination of buck infringement scents and doe-in-heat scents attracts the buck, either out of the urge to exert dominance or to breed.

During the primary breeding phase, set up along the buck's rub route, in areas does regularly use, or in travel corridors between doe core areas. Because the does are in estrus, the buck may be either with a doe or looking for one. If you know the buck is not with a doe and is staying in his traditional core area, set up as close to the core area as you can. Try to get between the buck and the first doe area he visits. If he finds an estrus doe before he gets to your stand site, chances are he will follow the doe and not his rub route. By setting up between the buck's core area and the first doe-use area it travels to, you have a good chance of seeing the buck on a regular basis and attracting it to your stand.

Because the buck is looking for does and wants to protect his breeding rights, both territorial/dominance scents and sex scents work. If you have previously patterned a buck and know where its core area is, you can set up near it to intercept him as he goes into it in the morning or as he leaves in the evening. You can employ the same

The proper use of scents can help you harvest a trophy-class buck like this one.

methods used during the scraping phase. If you don't know where the buck's core area is, and know that the buck may be on the prowl during the day, you can set up near dominance areas of scrapes and rub lines near doe feeding and core areas in the evening. I use several filled scent holders spread out to attract the buck over a wide area. If you know the buck is traveling late in the morning you can use these same techniques on the rub route back to his core area.

Remember that the buck may be traveling anywhere and anytime in search of does during the breeding period (peak rut). Because the buck is unpredictable at this time you should spend as much time as possible on stand. Hunt three or more days in each area, changing stand sites frequently. If the buck is with an estrus doe it will travel with her for up to three days and may not return to normal activities until she is out of estrus. If you quit hunting the area after two or three days you may miss the buck when he returns to his normal pattern.

Hunting a buck after the breeding phase can be extremely frustrating unless you know where the buck's core area is. After all the fighting, chasing and breeding of the rut, the buck is worn out, hungry and in need of food to supply enough fat to get him through the winter. He is going to look for a secure place to rest with high-quality food sources nearby. Between the first and the second breeding phases some bucks may not be seen because they rest up. If you know where their core area is, and where available food sources are, you can set up between the two to intercept a buck. By this time the bucks are not as willing to fight, but they are still interested in breeding, so estrus scents may work the best. Some bucks may respond to curiosity scents and food scents like acorn, corn and peanut butter.

Three to four weeks after the primary breeding phase there is usually a late breeding period. In many areas the bucks will start to travel their routes again two to three weeks after the end of the primary breeding period, traveling through doe-use areas and doe feeding sites in search of estrus does. Since most of the does have been bred, the bucks do a lot of wandering and searching. Because of the colder temperatures in some areas, the activity of the deer is dependent on the weather. They will travel during good weather, but stay in or near core areas during cold, damp, windy or very wet weather. Expect deer to move and feed for a couple of hours when warming occurs after a cold spell. Hunt buck core areas, nearby buck food sources, rub routes and doe core areas and feeding sites. Bucks respond well to sex, curiosity and food scents at this time.

After the rut the bucks again return to their core areas and seek out nutrient-rich food sources to put on weight for the winter. Because the rut is

RIGHT SCENT, RIGHT TIME

Fall is when deer search out quality food sources to put on enough fat to get them through the winter. It is also the breeding season. These are the two driving forces that stimulate deer in the fall. All deer travel more at this time in search of food. Bucks travel much more than normal while establishing dominance and trying to locate does. The different phases of the rut also signal increases and decreases in sexual interest. Remember that territorial/dominance scents may scare off subdominant bucks, especially during the scraping and breeding phases, when the dominant bucks are aggressive. If you are looking for any buck you may not want to use these scents.

Phase	Activity	Effective Scents
Pre-Rut/Rubbing	Bucks are looking for food and starting to become interested in breeding.	recognition/trailing, sex, territorial/dominance, food, curiosity
Pre-Primary Breeding/Scraping	Bucks are proclaiming dominance by establishing rubs and scrapes.	recognition/trailing, sex, territorial/dominance, food, curiosity
Primary Breeding and Post-Primary Breeding	Bucks are looking for does and protecting their breeding rights.	territorial/dominance and sex
Rest Phase	Bucks are not as willing to fight but are still interested in breeding.	curiosity, but food may work best
Pre-Late Breeding and Late Breeding	Bucks look for does that come into a late estrus.	sex, curiosity and food
Post-Rut Phase	Bucks are not aggressive and often travel together to feeding areas.	curiosity, food

over the bucks are not aggressive and often travel together to feeding areas. Though most of the does have been bred bucks will still respond to doe estrus scents. Curiosity and food scents can attract bucks near core areas, buck feeding sites, and travel lanes between the two.

Using Calls

Deer calls fall into five basic categories: alarm/distress, agonistic, maternal/neonatal, mating and contact. Alarm/distress, agonistic, and maternal/neonatal calls have limited use by their very nature. Contact calls are used by deer to let their presence be known and to locate other deer. They work well to attract deer at any time. Mating calls are used primarily during the rut and you can use them successfully at that time to attract deer.

Alarm and distress calls are used to alert other deer of danger or used by deer when they are injured, trapped or afraid. Alarm calls cause other deer to become cautious or come to the aid of the deer performing the call. The alarm snort is used to alert other deer of possible danger—usually when a deer sees, smells or hears a predator or something unknown. I use the alarm snort when a deer snorts or stamps its foot after it discovers me, or when it is alarmed by the sight, scent or sound of me. If the deer does not immediately flee I snort back, imitating another alarmed deer. Deer that hear a snort in response to their own snort often mistake the sight or sound that alerted them for another deer (as long as they don't smell danger). I have had does with fawns come to my snort call, wanting to discover the deer they thought they heard. They often walk into the open for a better look, and stand long enough for a shot. Snorts can also be used while rattling to simulate a fight. The distress bawl is used by deer that are hurt or trapped. The bawl is a call for help and may attract maternal does and sometimes young bucks out of curiosity. I have had does leave their own young to investigate a long drawn-out distress bawl.

The maternal and neonatal calls are used by the doe and its fawns to communicate with each other. The maternal grunt sounds much like any other grunt, and will attract any deer, especially bucks during the rut. The fawn mew, bleat and nursing whine may attract does out of maternal instinct, and young deer or small bucks out of curiosity.

The agonistic calls express dominance or submission. The grunt is the first level of aggression, but it is used by all deer regularly and will attract any deer—especially bucks of all ages—throughout the rut. The grunt-snort is the next level of aggression and is used primarily by bucks during the breeding season in buck encounters. Because it often occurs when two bucks are in conflict over an estrus doe, it will attract bucks, especially dominants, from the time velvet is shed until the end of the second breeding phase. The grunt-snort can be used in conjunction with rattling to simulate a fight or a buck making a rage rub. The grunt-snort-wheeze is the highest level of aggression and is performed primarily by bucks before a charge, leg kick or fight. It may scare off lesser bucks, while attracting a dominant when used near its rubs and scrapes, or it can be used to stop a buck with an estrus doe. The grunt-snort-wheeze is best used when hunting only for dominant bucks, from the time they shed their velvet through the late breeding period.

Because mating calls are associated with breeding, they may attract any buck looking for a doe, especially dominants wanting to find out what other buck is in the area. The tending grunt is performed when a buck is following or with an estrus doe to warn all other bucks to stay away. I have heard bucks make one short grunt (while with a doe), several grunts (almost with every stride), and a long drawn-out (seven-second) grunt while trotting after a doe. A buck performs the Flehmen sniff when it is inhaling urine odor to check for estrogen, often while trailing or with a doe. Because both the tending grunt and the Flehmen sniff indicate a nearby estrus doe, any buck in the area may respond throughout the rut, especially dominants. However, young bucks may avoid the area of this call, fearing an encounter with a dominant buck.

Determining what call to use when you are hunting white-tailed deer is not a matter of which rut phase you are hunting, but which sex and age class of deer you want to attract. Does respond to distress calls and maternal and neonatal calls primarily out of maternal instinct. All bucks respond to any call, which may lead them to an estrus doe, a social grunt or low grunt. Dominant bucks also respond to mating calls and aggressive grunts out of the desire to exert dominance. Subdominant bucks may respond to these same calls during the breeding phase, but they may not respond because they are afraid of encountering a dominant. If you are hunting for any legal buck it may be best not to use mating calls or aggressive grunts.

There are basically four different techniques for calling deer that can be used anytime during the rut.

- For does and possibly young bucks: Distress Call/Fawn Bawl, with Trailing/Recognition scent, and a doe decoy.
- For does and bucks: Social or Low Grunt, with Food, Curiosity, and Trailing/Recognition scent, and a doe decoy.
- For any buck: Social/Low/Tending Grunt, with rattling/thrashing, Trailing/Recognition and doe urine/estrus scents, and a doe decoy.
- For dominant bucks: Social/Low/Tending Grunt/Grunt Snort, with rattling/thrashing, Trailing/ Recognition and Territorial/ Dominance and estrus scents, and either a buck or doe decoy.

All of these combined techniques can be used anytime during the rut. The fourth technique is not as effective during the Rest Phase and Post-Rut because the bucks are exhausted and not as interested in breeding. Doe-in-heat scents and buck urine are suggested because they can be used anytime during the rut, and they work better to attract bucks than simple doe urine.

The contact call or social grunt is by nature non-threatening, because it is used to locate other deer. Any deer may respond out of curiosity, especially bucks, throughout the rut. In Marchinton's study no doe-in-heat or doe breeding call was noted, although many call manufacturers contend there is one. The sound of the call they claim is an estrus doe bleat may actually be the social grunt, which is louder and longer than normal and is used to locate other deer, therefore it attracts bucks during the rut.

Rattling

Prior to and during the rut, bucks rub on trees, thrash brush, and participate in sparring matches to establish dominance. Dominant bucks encountering each other, especially if an estrus doe is near, may fight for breeding rights. The sounds of any of these activities (rubbing, thrashing, sparring and fighting) may attract other bucks in the area, particularly dominants. Subdominants that have previously been beaten in a fight may immediately leave the area. Rattling is most effective in areas with high buck to doe ratios. It is also effective in areas with high numbers of dominant bucks, in areas with limited habitat, such as urban areas, in the marginal habitat of prairie river bottoms, and in areas managed for trophy quality.

I have rattled bucks from as far away as ½ mile (0.8 km) using loud, long sequences. It took the bucks an average of 20 minutes to come in from downwind. I have also had bucks 40 yards (36 m) away run all the way to my stand, and I brought the bucks back when they began to leave. However, I found that if a buck doesn't find a deer when it responds to rattling it may not respond to rattling in the same location more than twice. Don't rattle the same buck from the same stand twice on successive days. If he comes in but you didn't get him wait three to four days before trying again.

Bucks respond to rattling out of curiosity and dominance. They want to find out which bucks are fighting and if there is an estrus doe with them. Rattle near areas bucks regularly use: buck feeding/sparring areas, buck bedrooms, doe feeding and staging areas, and dominance areas of rubs and scrapes.

In a comprehensive three-year study by researchers from the University of Georgia and Texas A & M–Kingsville, deer responded in 65 percent of 171 rattling sessions. In 73 percent of the responses bucks came to loud, long rattling, which worked best in the pre-rut. Loud, short rattling worked best during peak rut. Quiet, long rattling worked best in post-rut (slightly more mature [3½-year-old] bucks responded).

The highest number of responses occurred during peak rut, when most bucks were active. Middle-aged 3½ to 4½-year-old bucks responded best for the entire rut. During the pre-rut 1½- to 2½-year-old bucks responded best. Older bucks responded equally well during the pre-rut and post-rut, but less during peak rut (probably because they were with or searching for does). Bucks responded more deliberately and slowly during post-rut. The bucks usually responded during the first of three 10-minute rattling sessions.

How long and how loud you rattle can determine your "rattling success rate" during the different phases of the rut.

T.R.'S KEYPOINTS

During the pre-rut, use long, loud rattling sequences to attract wide ranging bucks.

During peak rut, when the bucks are most active, use short, loud rattling sequences. Long rattling sequences make you prone to discovery.

During post-rut use quiet, long rattling sequences. Bucks are not as aggressive after the rut and don't travel as much; give them time to respond.

The best responses occurred when wind speed was lowest, responses decreased as wind speed increased. The highest response rates also occurred when cloud cover was about 75 percent. Lowest rates occurred when skies were clear. Two thirds of the bucks were first spotted downwind. Morning sessions produced the highest number of responses, but older bucks responded more in the afternoon.

If bucks are not nearby, the initial contact of the antlers should be loud to get their attention. When the bucks are nearby, rattle softer.

When you rattle loudly bring the racks together with a crash, then roll your wrists and grind the racks together, simulating two bucks pushing and shoving each other for one to three minutes. Then stop and listen for a buck's approach for three to five minutes before beginning again.

Remember: Before leaving the stand site check the area thoroughly, especially if you have been watching a deer. More than one buck may have responded and be nearby.

In a test of radio-collared deer, it was determined that the best time to rattle for mature bucks was during the post-rut. The researchers believed that young bucks were bunched up at that time and were more interested in feeding than fighting. Mature bucks remain aggressive well after the primary breeding period has ended. The researchers believed that the second best time to rattle mature bucks was during the pre-rut. Even though bucks may be bunched up at this time, it is usually the dominant buck that responds.

Because the test deer were radio collared, the rattler was able to set up within 200 to 300 yards (182 to 273 m) of the buck's location to be sure the deer could hear the rattling. About 20 to 25 percent of the bucks during this study responded after the third one- to three-minute rattling sequence, a full 20 minutes into the session. As a result of this it was recommended that hunters who rattle wait 30 minutes before giving up or moving to a new location. During the study trophy bucks responded 75 percent of the time, while smaller bucks responded 50 percent of the time. When responding to rattling, 65 percent of the bucks made their final approach from downwind. However, the study showed that the rattler saw only about half the bucks that responded.

T.R.'S KEYPOINTS

Rattling works best in the morning when bucks are still searching for does or heading for core areas. It is less effective during midday when bucks are bedded. Older dominant bucks may respond best in the evening.

Bucks that respond to rattling are intent on discovering the source, which leaves you vulnerable to discovery. Take precautions to conceal or disguise unnatural sights, scents, sounds and you from the deer.

Hang a second set of antlers from your tree stand. When bucks get close, these antlers can be jerked and rattled, keeping movement to a minimum and away from you.

Rustling leaves, pounding the ground with a stick or rattling racks, and grunting and blowing add realism to the sound of rattling and thrashing.

Larger antlers and some imitation racks work best because their sound carries farther. Be sure to use racks with a neutral color so the deer doesn't easily notice them.

If a buck shows up, but won't come into range, rattle softly while it can't see you, or use a grunt call to coax it into range.

If the buck starts to leave before you get a shot, or won't hold still, use a grunt call to stop it.

Decoying Deer

Deer decoys have been around in some form for a long time. There is evidence that Native Americans used hides to cover themselves to avoid detection and attract deer at the same time. In modern days, deer silhouettes have been used for many years. Hunters successfully use full mounted deer, archery targets, fiberglass, plastic and collapsible foam decoys. Because I guide and carry a lot of gear, any product must meet certain requirements. It must work, be lightweight, compact and portable.

I first got the idea for a collapsible deer decoy when I saw a hunter promoting the use of a full-mounted bedded doe decoy at the Minnesota Deer Classic in the early 1990s. He said he'd been using the decoy for about a year, and had good success luring bucks to it during the archery season. While I thought the idea was good I foresaw a few problems with it. Many of the places I hunted, were in the bluff and coulee country along the Mississippi River. It would be too heavy, too bulky and too noisy to carry any farther than a few yards (meters). To reach most of the places I hunted I had to walk more than a ¼ mile (0.4 km). What I needed was a lightweight compact decoy,

Proper placement of deer decoys can help you get the best shot on the deer of your choice.

one that could be carried in a backpack or over my shoulder.

Since I had already come up with the idea for a full-bodied goose decoy for Feather Flex, I called them and told them I wanted them to take a deer taxidermy form, make a mold out of it, and use the cross-linked foam they used on their turkey and goose decoys to make a bedded deer decoy. I told them I'd also like to see detachable antlers on it, so it could be used as either a buck or a doe. And if they changed the color and pattern of the decoy they could use it as a mule deer, elk calf and a pronghorn. Although it was a bedded decoy it easily made up for lack its lack of high profile in its portability and ease of use. What good is a decoy if you can't get it there?

Six months after I came up with the idea I received three of the first decoys to field test. After using the decoys for a year, I learned when, where and how to use them. During my research I encountered a couple of areas where the decoy should not be used. I placed it directly on a deer trail, where deer would not normally bed. A six-point buck that came to a grunt call really checked out the doe decoy. He stayed within 15 yards (13 m) of the decoy for ten minutes. I could have easily taken him several times as he walked around the area. But he never came closer than 10 yards (9 m). He came closest when he smelled the doe scent from downwind, but was reluctant to come closer because the decoy was in an unnatural area. For best results put a bedded decoy in areas where a deer might normally lie down. Standing decoys can be used on or near trails.

I also placed the decoy just off the trail, near a scrape, in a bottleneck leading to a feeding area. The first deer to see it was a doe with two fawns. When I first saw her I grunted to get her attention. She looked up, spotted the decoy, stared, then slowly fed toward the decoy. It took her 15 minutes to cover 20 yards (18 m), all the while stopping to look at the decoy. I was on the ground, not 10 yards (9 m) from the decoy, when a big-bodied, 140-class eight-point buck came up behind me. Before I heard him he was within 10 yards (9 m) of the decoy and staring. Then I

heard more movement and five does and fawns moved up behind the buck. They all looked at the decoy then moved around it before approaching the doe with her fawns coming from the other direction. Then they ran through the bottleneck avoiding the other doe.

It was obvious the five does and fawns had avoided the bedded decoy and wanted to go through the bottleneck but were reluctant while the other doe and her fawns were on the trail. They were passing through the home range of the first doe, which was one of the dominants in the area and she had priority. They avoided the decoy because they couldn't identify it but they were not alarmed and approached within 10 yards (9 m) of the decoy.

Does were not as curious as bucks and seldom came closer than 10 yards (9 m). The decoy did not threaten them but did not arouse any dominance or breeding activity as it did in bucks. Eventually all these deer passed within 10 yards (9 m) of the decoy. Most of them stopped long enough and close enough that I could have taken every one of them. Although the does showed little interest other than curiosity, the buck stood long enough to get a good whiff of the estrus scent. Because he was with an estrus doe he decided to attend to the business at hand. I watched later as he drove the fawns away and began chasing the doe.

When the decoy was placed in other areas, bucks would come up and kick the decoy to initiate breeding. On one video the buck actually rolled a decoy with small antlers 20 yards (18 m). But even if these close encounters didn't happen it wouldn't have mattered. The decoy brought deer close enough to shoot, positioned them for a clear shot, and stopped them long enough to get a shot. At the same time it distracted their attention from my position so that I could easily raise my gun or bow and shoot.

Hunters have reservations and questions about the use of deer decoys, such as: Are they legal? Do they work? Where do you put them? When can you use them? When should you use them?

As far as I know, decoys are legal everywhere. There has been talk of regulating them in some states, but I don't know of any state where they have been banned. I think one of the major concerns has been safety. That can be addressed by hanging a red cloth or orange flagging near the decoy. Do they work? The answer to that question is an unequivocal "sometimes." When used in the right area, at the right time, and precautions taken that no unnatural sight, scent or sound is associated with the decoy they can be very effective.

Where and How to Use Decoys

Decoys work best in high-use areas where deer are seen on a regular basis. If you hunt bucks then the decoy should be placed along buck travel routes, in bottlenecks, in staging areas near food sources or near the dominance areas of rubs and scrapes bucks frequent on a regular basis. The decoy also needs to be within the hunter's shooting distance, in a shooting lane and preferably not in a line from the deer to the hunter. When it is placed away from your stand site, the decoy can actually distract the deer's attention from you, giving you the opportunity to move and shoot.

I've found that mature bucks often hang up on the far side of the decoy out of range. But if I place a decoy 10 to 15 yards (9 to 13 m) slightly behind my shooting position, and the buck does hang up beyond the decoy, it is still in range. Since I am right-handed I prefer to place a decoy off to my left side, because it is easier for me to shoot in front and to the left than it is to the extreme right. I also like to place the decoy either directly to my left or slightly behind me.

Decoys can be used any time of the year. Both bucks and does may respond to any new deer in their area out of curiosity, often wanting to get within a few yards of a new deer or decoy on the downwind side—so they can scent-check it. Any deer may respond to a decoy at dawn and dusk along travel lanes, in bottlenecks and near feeding areas, simply because that's where the deer are at those times of the day, and that is when they are most active. Bucks may respond to decoys anytime during the day between the time peak scraping begins until the end of the primary

If you are after trophy bucks only, you may want to use a buck decoy with large antlers like this one. However, remember that the large antlers on this decoy may scare off subdominant bucks.

breeding phase, because they are often active all day long during those phases. They may be active all day long again during the late breeding phase.

Bucks respond well to doe decoys during most phases of the rut, especially when the decoy is used in conjunction with calls, scents and rattling, because bucks are interested in breeding as long as they have hard antlers. Bucks of all ages respond best to buck decoys with small antlers during the pre-rut/rubbing phase, dispersal/fall home range shift phase, early breeding/scraping phase and primary breeding phase, because they want to know what other bucks are in their areas.

You may be able to position a buck for a shot, because bucks often approach other bucks and does differently. Since bucks often approach does from the side or rear, to check the doe for breeding readiness, you should place a doe decoy with its rump toward you or facing to your right or left. This should present you with a side shot of the buck when it approaches the doe decoy. Because bucks often approach other bucks cautiously from the front, you should place a buck decoy with its head toward you or facing to your right or left. This should present you with a side shot of the buck as it moves toward the front of the buck decoy. You should not place the decoy in a direct line between you and where you expect the deer to come from, because the deer may see you as they come in. Place the decoy off to one side of your stand to distract the deer's attention from your position.

If you are interested in bucks with antlers of any size, you should not use decoys with large antlers. Large antlers may keep younger or small-racked bucks from responding. Conversely, if you want to attract only older, large-racked bucks you may want to use decoys with large racks, so the decoy won't attract younger bucks. You can increase the visibility of the decoy by placing it in open areas or on a log or bush. You can use standing full-bodied or silhouette decoys. You can also use standing and bedded decoys in combination.

T.R.'S KEYPOINTS

Don't get human or unnatural scent on the decoy. Use gloves when carrying and positioning the decoy, then spray it with cover-up scent.

Don't place bedded decoys directly on trails. Deer don't usually bed on trails.

Place decoys upwind of where you expect the deer to appear. Bucks like to approach downwind from cover if they can.

Place a doe decoy with its rump toward you. Bucks often approach does from the rear or side, presenting you with a shot.

Place a buck decoy with its head toward you for a shot. Bucks generally approach another buck cautiously from the front.

To get the buck's attention on the decoy, tape a small piece of white plastic to the tail area, so that it can blow in the wind, or use one of the new tail motion decoys.

To keep the buck's attention focused on the decoy place a few drops of deer urine on it—doe-in-estrus for doe decoys, buck-in-rut for buck decoys.

Why Decoys Do and Don't Work

Deer respond to calls, scents, rattling and decoys, and may come into range because they were going in that direction anyway. They were attracted by a sight, scent or sound, or they were just plain curious. When deer respond to scents, calls or rattling, but hang up out of shooting range, it's often because they don't see another deer. In order to survive the deer have to rely on their senses. To attract deer you have to convince them that one of their own kind is where you want them to be by using the "3 Ss"—sight, scent and sound. The addition of a decoy to calls, rattling and scents completes the total illusion of a real animal in the area.

Deer don't respond to decoys or come into range when they smell, hear or see something that is not natural. They don't want to go to the area where the hunter is or they hear or smell another deer but don't see it. When you use a decoy, be sure to keep the decoy free of any unnatural odors, use products to reduce all unnatural odors on you and your clothing, and wear rubber gloves and boots when you set up you decoy, so you do not contaminate the area.

If a wary buck is traveling through the area where you hunt and hears your grunt call or rattling, smells your deer scent, and is in the mood—it may come in to investigate. But if it doesn't see another deer it may not come into range. If it comes to the decoy just because it is curious and wants to find out what this new thing is, it may present a closer shot than if you were not using a decoy. And that is why you use any product that attracts deer—to get the animal into range, no matter what the reason.

As with anything else in deer hunting you should always play the wind. I've found that bucks often respond to scents, calls and rattling by trying to come in from downwind—if they can. The same can be said for decoys. Bucks often want to scent-check a decoy before they come in to it. For this reason be sure you set up in an area where the buck can approach the decoy without scenting you from directly downwind. I like to set up so that, if the buck wants to come in downwind, it has only one way that offers cover. Because I am right-handed I like the cover, or the route the buck is most likely to use, to be on my left side.

CHAPTER 7

Hunting Sites

A stand is where you choose to hunt. It can be any location where you wait for the animals: near a tree, a rock or a hilltop; in a tree stand, a tripod or a ground blind. The main purpose of a stand is to allow you to see the animal and get a shot before it detects you. A stand site should afford some means of protection from the animal seeing, smelling or hearing you, while letting you see the animal.

Your method of hunting dictates where you place your stand. If you are rifle or muzzleloader hunting, your stand can be farther away from where you expect deer than if you are shotgun, handgun, archery or crossbow hunting. Distance alone is enough to avoid detection. The shorter the effective range of you and your weapon, the more concealment from sight and sound, and the more the wind direction dictates where your stand should be placed. If you intend to wait for the animals or use techniques to attract them at distances closer than 100 yards (91 m), place your stand out of the direct line of sight of the animal and keep downwind or crosswind from its approach. A tree stand can be placed near high-use areas, but can be out of normal visual range because of height. Height also helps to disperse scent and sound.

Ground stands can be effective as long as adequate concealment or camouflage is used, and precautions are taken so the animal doesn't smell you. There are numerous hunting blinds that conceal movement, muffle sound and, because you are out of the wind, prevent smell from escaping. Because deer have learned to look into trees for hunters and associate the upright human form with danger, I have begun hunting more from the ground. The biggest advantages of ground stand hunting are mobility and comfort. By sitting on rocks, logs, the ground or my Back Seat portable stool, I can easily pick up and move if the area is unproductive. I don't have to worry about hanging multiple stands that may or may not be in the right location, or taking down my stand and moving it. I simply get up and walk away. This is especially helpful if there is a sudden wind change.

While I am sitting on my stool I don't present the upright human form, and deer don't perceive me as a danger. I have been hunting from ground stands for years and have had more close encounters with animals and shooting opportunities than I have when hunting from a tree stand.

Tree Stands

There are too many brands and models of tree stands to mention, but one of the best stands I have used comes from Buck Finder. Most stands need a tree that is fairly straight. The seat of the Buck Finder Dominator has a swivel at the base that can be adjusted to fit a tree even if it leans forward, backward or sideways. One of the things I like about these stands is that they hang on a screw-in J-hook or a strap with a J-hook attached to it. When I want to move my stand I take it off the J-hook and move it to another J-hook I already have in place. Because of its light weight I can easily carry in a Non-Typical or a Lone Wolf stand and two ladders, and be ready to hunt in a few minutes. Several different stand manufacturers offer a variety of portable seats, seats and platforms, slings and climbing stands. They also offer a variety of climbing sticks and ladder/platforms.

The author is careful to use a climbing belt as he hangs his deer stand. Once he is in his stand he will use a safety belt.

With hunters spending so much time in tree stands hoping to see and get a shot at a deer, the location of the stand in relation to where they expect to see the deer is crucial. I often see stands hung too close to open feeding areas or too far from core areas; too far from, or too close to, deer travel corridors and trails; in places where the wind or thermal currents are wrong; in surroundings where the hunter is sky-lined; and often too low.

Stand Location

In order for you to get the most out of your tree stand, it needs to be in the right location—an area frequented by deer at the time of the day that you intend to hunt. Ideally, this is in a wooded or semi-wooded area where the deer feel secure during the day. Since deer spend the majority of the daylight hours in secure areas, often in thick vegetation and wooded or low-lying areas where visibility is limited, the majority of your stand sites should be in or near those areas. If you can't see the deer and shoot into those areas, you are too far away. Deer, especially older bucks, don't usually leave their security areas and move into open areas until shortly before or after sunset. This means that hunters who place their stands at the edge of agricultural fields and other open areas will see fewer deer, especially older bucks, during legal hunting hours, than hunters who place their stands in or near the secure areas.

A stand also needs to be close enough to where you expect to see the deer to get a shot, but far enough away so that the deer don't detect you while you are waiting or getting ready for a shot. Obviously hunters using a bow, crossbow, handgun, shotgun or muzzleloader need to be closer to the deer than a rifle hunter. When you choose a location for your stand consider the effective shooting distance of you and your weapon, then set up several yards closer than that for good measure. Do not set your stand too close to where you expect to see the deer. Too often I see stands that are within yards of a deer trail, or are hanging off to the side of the trail where the deer may be looking directly toward the stand as it comes around a corner in the trail. If you are using a short-range weapon, and can see several yards (meters) of the trail in any one direction, you are probably too close.

Although you want to be close to the deer's core area, where it spends most of its time during daylight hours, you don't want to be so close that you alert the deer to your presence. You don't want the deer to smell, hear or see you when you put your stand up (which is when you can be seen, smelled or heard by the deer as you walk in, hang your stand and clear shooting lanes) or you are in it. How close you can get to the core area depends on the terrain, the thickness of the vegetation and the wind direction. No matter what the terrain and vegetation are like, I don't think you can set

TIME OF DAY CHOICES

An understanding of deer behavior and travel patterns helps when choosing a hunting site. Because deer feed primarily during low light conditions they have two primary rest periods: within a couple of hours of sunrise and within a couple hours of sunset. Generally they leave their daytime core areas in heavy cover during the late afternoon and move toward nighttime food sources. They intermittently feed, travel and rest during the night before returning to their daytime core areas the next morning.

Because the amount of light is a security factor, deer in forested areas get up and begin to feed and move a couple of hours before sundown. As it becomes darker the deer move into more open areas of low brush or sparse forest and feed, moving toward open fields and meadows. Shortly before sundown they move into the shadows at the edges of tall grass and swamps before going into open meadows or agricultural fields where they feel secure and feed during darkness.

In the early morning this pattern is reversed. As the sky begins to brighten the deer move from the open areas back into tall grass fields, then to brushy areas just before daylight, and into heavy cover or woods once the sun is up. Bucks are generally more wary than does and move about half an hour later in the evening, and head back to their beds about half an hour earlier in the morning.

Evening Stands

If you are hunting late in the afternoon, when the deer are just getting out of their beds in heavy cover, set up along travel lanes leading from the core areas to daytime food sources, near small openings in woods, fallen mast sites, and swamp or creek edges near heavy cover. Close to sundown, hunt the transition zones of tall grass, heavy brush, swamps and gullies. Trails leading to staging areas, downwind of open food sources are excellent at sundown, especially for bucks.

If you are hunting at or after sundown, and the deer are feeding in the open, your stand should be along trails leading to the fields. Bucks move later than does and often come into the transition zones after sundown. They prefer to stay in cover until sundown, when they feel secure. If you don't see bucks in open feeding areas, move farther into the woods along buck travel routes in heavy cover and forested areas. Because the deer move late in the evening you have plenty of time to get to staging areas and transition zones before they arrive.

Morning Stands

In the early morning, when the deer are still feeding in the open, don't hunt from stands near open night food sources, unless you are sure there are no deer near your stand or you can approach it undetected. Because of the darkness, you won't know if there are deer in the area until it's too late. If you spook a deer it will alert all the others in the area. Hunt transition zones, heavy cover where deer travel on their way from feeding areas, or trails leading to core areas. Be at your stand before the deer and ambush them on their return.

Before the breeding phase, bucks usually return to cover well before daylight. Hunt rub routes back to the buck bedroom early in the morning, getting there before the buck. Once the rut begins, the bucks may return later than normal because they are either chasing or looking for does. Early in the morning, you may catch the buck along his rub route near transition zones on the way back to the core area. If the buck is not in his core area, hunt near it from first light until noon. I have seen bucks drag themselves home at 11:00 a.m. If you have previously observed or patterned a buck you will know when and where the best setup is.

up a stand closer than 100 yards (91 m) without the deer hearing, seeing or smelling you. Air currents often determine where you can set up, because wind from you to the core area will carry your scent to the deer. If the wind or thermals are wrong, ¼ mile (0.4 km) may be too close.

Wind and Thermal Currents

One of the most important considerations in tree stand placement should be wind direction and the movement of thermal air currents. You want to place your stand where it is either downwind of where you expect to see deer, or down- and crosswind of the direction in which you think the deer will be moving. You don't want the deer to be able to smell you, if at all possible, when you are hunting, even if you don't get a shot. If you have to set up crosswind of a deer's approach, you should be very confident that you will be able to take the deer when it comes by, and that the deer won't cross your downwind scent until it is well past you, which should be out of range. If a deer smells you, even if you didn't get a shot, it may leave behind enough interdigital or metatarsal scent to alarm other deer that may come through the area. Those warning scents may linger for hours, reducing your chances of seeing any deer as long as you are there.

You also need to take into consideration the effects of thermal currents. If you hunt in country with gullies, ravines, hills or mountains, there is a good chance that changing thermal currents will not allow you to hunt some stands at particular times of the day. Thermal currents generally rise in the morning as the sun heats up the air, and fall in the evening as the air cools. When the wind is blowing, these thermal currents might not be noticeable while you are hunting and they may not affect your hunting. Thermal currents may not be noticeable even when there is no wind, but they can ruin a stand location just as easily as the wind.

When you set up your stand, be aware of the terrain and the vegetation. Thick trees (especially evergreens) in otherwise less dense areas may funnel the wind and thermal currents into some areas. If the area you hunt has changes in elevation, think about what time of day you want

Stands can be movable or permanent, small or large, depending on how much time you hunt one area.

to hunt the area, and which way the thermals may be moving at that time of day. If you are unsure whether or not there are thermals in the area, use talcum powder, thistle down, a piece of sewing thread tied to your weapon, or a commercial product like Breeze Detector from Wildlife Research Center to determine when and which direction the thermals are blowing.

Stand Placement

When you set up your stand you don't want to be sky-lined, or noticeable from a deer's level of sight. Try to place your stand in a tree as wide as your body, or with other trees, limbs or a hill behind you. The denser the background behind you, the harder it will be for the deer to spot you. When I hang a stand I pick a spot on the tree, and go to where I think I will have my shots, and squat down so that I'm at the level of the deer. I then look at the spot I picked to hang my stand. If I see a lot of sky, I know I have chosen the wrong spot. It may also be beneficial to hunt with the sun behind you, rather than in your face, where and when it is possible. Having the sun behind you keeps sunlight from glaring off you and your equipment, and it makes it easier to see in front of you.

There are two main things you have to consider when you hang a stand: the strength and straightness of the tree. The tree needs to be big enough to support the combined weight of you and your stand. Even if a tree is big enough to hold you it may be cracked or rotten, but it needs to be healthy so it will hold together in a high wind. Check the tree carefully, to make sure there are no cracks or rotted areas in it, and give it a good thump with your tree steps or a stick to make sure it sounds solid. If you have screw-in steps you also need to make sure you can get your steps into the tree.

Another consideration in stand placement is how high off the ground you want to be. Height alone can keep you out of the normal line of sight of the deer. Depending on the terrain and vegetation where you hunt, and the speed and direction of the wind or thermal currents, if you are high enough, the air currents may keep your scent above the areas. On the other hand, if you are producing scents that can be detected by the deer, and there is no wind, the higher you are, the more your scent spreads out around you as it descends. One drawback to height is that the higher you are, the smaller your target zone gets, especially if you are using a short-range weapon. The side of a deer offers a lot bigger target at ground level than the top of a deer.

You should also think about the terrain around you when you choose a height for your stand. If you hunt steep hills and ravines, and the deer are moving below you, there is no need to place your stand 20 feet (6 m) up in a tree, because the deer may already be 5 to 20 feet (1.5 to 6 m) below your stand. On the other hand, if you hunt in hilly country or in a ravine or gully, and the deer move on higher ground than your tree, you may have to put your stand higher than normal, because the deer may be moving at about the same level as your stand. When you place your stand remember that one of the purposes of using a tree stand is to be above the normal line of sight of the deer around you, no matter high you are.

While I am on the ground checking to see if my stand is sky-lined, I also check to see if I have one or more clear shooting lanes from my stand.

If I don't, I decide whether or not I can cut off some limbs and clear brush out of the area to create shooting lanes. If I have to remove too much vegetation, I look for another place to hang my stand. Cutting too many branches and removing too much brush may be noticeable to the deer and they may be alert when they approach the area. If they discover a sight, scent or sound that is out of place the first time they come through the area, they may spook, take another route or travel after dark. You can avoid this by putting your stand up two weeks or so in advance, and then staying out of the area until you plan to hunt. That way the deer have a chance to get accustomed to the changes when you aren't there, and without the sight, scent or sound of you.

Once I've hung my stands (I often hang two or three stands in the same area so I can hunt according to the air currents) I look for one or more routes I can use to get to it. The route I use depends on the time of day I hunt, which direction the air currents are moving, and where I expect the deer to be as I go to my stand. I like to use the easiest route I can find, one where I don't have to walk through a lot of brush that I might leave scent on as I walk by. I avoid rough or steep terrain if I can, so that I don't have to work too hard to get where I'm going, which may cause me to make a lot of noise or to work up a sweat.

Unless I have spent a lot of time in the area, and the deer have gotten accustomed to seeing, smelling and hearing me moving through it, I try to stay well away from any deer trail, especially the lightly used buck trails and rub routes. If I have to cross a trail I try to do it far enough from where I expect the deer to be coming from, and far enough in advance of the time they get there, that much of my scent will have dispersed by the time the deer come through. If there are watercourses in the area that I can walk in, I use them to get to my stand. However, because I often scout my hunting areas every day, checking for tracks, droppings and scrapes, the deer get used to me, which allows me to walk on or next to their trails without them becoming alarmed when I hunt. I believe that if you scout your hunting area two to three times per week, between 11:00 a.m. and 2:00 p.m., when the deer are usually in their core areas, you can get the deer accustomed to your scent and you can use the same trails the deer do when you go to your stand.

Tree Stand Safety

Safety should be on your mind every time you get into your tree stand. All too often, hunters fail to use even the slightest precautions when they are in their stands. Climbing 10 to 20 feet (3 to 6 m) up a tree on tree steps, and standing on a 2- to 4-foot square (0.18 to 0.36 square m) platform that high up is dangerous; take some precautions so that you, or someone you are with doesn't fall and get hurt. Use a climbing belt when you go up the tree, and a safety belt or harness when you are in the tree. Two of my favorite safety belts are the Treehopper, which doubles as a heavy duty climbing and safety belt, and the Silent Slide safety belt, which allows you to pivot 180° in silence.

When my kids took up hunting I began to worry about their safety. I firmly believe that a safety harness is the best precaution you can take, especially if you are a heavy person, or for children.

Ground Blinds, the Forgotten Deer Stand

Some whitetail hunters are so accustomed to hunting from tree stands in wooded areas that they forget there are other ways and other places to hunt deer. This is especially true of archery hunters. A look at the 1995 to 1996 Pope & Young Club book shows that of 3,670 archery hunters polled, over 75 percent hunted from tree stands. By limiting themselves to hunting from tree stands in wooded areas both archery and gun hunters may miss out on some the best places to hunt deer: harvested agricultural fields, scrub brush, open creek and river bottoms, rolling hills and prairies. Because so many deer hunters prefer to hunt in the woods, these open areas often receive little hunting pressure. As a result of this, many open areas harbor good numbers of bucks, some of them with large racks. The numbers of recent trophies taken from the open farm country of Illinois, Iowa, Kansas, and the scrub brush of Texas are a testament to the fact that big deer live in open areas.

Deer hunters place their tree stands up high so that they have a clear view of as much of the

Ground blinds like this Double Bull can put you in range of a buck when there are no suitable trees for a tree stand.

surrounding area as possible, while they keep themselves out of the deer's line of sight. In many cases being high up in a tree also reduces the amount of human scent on the ground near the hunters stand.

So, how do you accomplish these three things when hunting where there aren't any trees big enough to hang a stand? Use a ground blind. Placing a ground blind in a field, or on a hill overlooking a gully, or river or creek bottom, allows you to see much more country than a stand in most wooded areas does. It also keeps you out of the line of sight of the deer, keeps you far away enough from the deer that your scent dissipates, keeps your scent from blowing around. A blind can also keep you warm and dry, something those of us who hunt in the northern states in November and December really appreciate.

A ground blind can be as simple as a tree, bush, rock, hill or other natural feature. It can be as easy as using existing vegetation to create a blind or as comfortable as using a portable or permanent blind. During the years I guided for elk and mule deer in Colorado, Montana and New Mexico, my hunters and I often sat high on a hill near a rock, brush pile or tree while we surveyed the country looking for game. Sitting up high allowed us to watch as large of an area as possible, while remaining out of sight of animals below us, sitting by natural cover allowed us a to remain inconspicuous to animals that might be close by. Most of the big bulls the hunters took were shot from where we sat, and several of those shots were within 100 yards (91 m). Those shots could have been taken with the same rifles whitetail hunters use, with a handgun, or even a shotgun fitted with a rifled barrel and a variable power scope and using a high-powered Sabot slug.

Blind Placement

When I know bucks are crossing between two wooded fingers on either side of a corn, soybean or alfalfa field I place a blind 10 to 15 yards (9 to 14 m) from the crossing and close enough to one side of the field that I have a shot

when the buck shows itself. If the field is short enough, I can cover both sides of it. For gun hunting I like to set up a blind 50 to 60 yards (45 to 55 m) away from the inside corner of a field surrounded by trees. That way I can easily watch two sides of the field at the same time, especially the corner where bucks often seem to exit and enter the field, and where they often have a scrape. If I can, I set the blind up on a high spot in the field so that I can see as much of the field as possible. If I see deer that aren't in range, I move the blind closer for the next hunt. Moving the blind usually doesn't bother deer in farm country because they're used to seeing cars, pickups, tractors, combines and grain wagons sitting in fields in the fall.

When I'm hunting open gullies and river and creek bottoms, I place the blind on a bench, at the top of the hill or near the creek bed. I try to set it up a few days in advance of the hunt so the animals get used to it. Deer that frequent open plains and river and creek bottoms, especially in the plains states, aren't as accustomed to seeing vehicles and machinery as farm country deer are, and are more likely to avoid areas where something new shows up. For this same reason I try to place the blind in a brushy or grassy area, or on the side of the hill—someplace where it won't stand out against the sky and won't be easily seen by passing deer. I also keep the blind out of areas where the wind, and the rising and falling thermals, may send any scent that escapes from the blind to the animals.

Ground blinds can also be used by archery hunters while using scents, calls and decoys to bring in whitetails. Because of the shorter effective range of a bow, a blind used for archery hunting has to be placed closer to the specific areas that deer use. When I want to get close to a whitetail, I place my blinds in or at the ends of a bottleneck. Semi-open or wooded river and creek bottoms, brushy gullies, low wooded areas between two wooded hills, wooded saddles at the top of hills, or wooded fingers are excellent places to set up an archery blind. Two of the biggest bucks I've ever seen were within 10 yards (9 m) of my blind in wooded fingers.

To help break up the outline of your ground blind, place it in or near ground vegetation, and attach some of the vegetation to the blind.

The type of portable blind you use depends on how you hunt, how much protection from the elements you want, how far you may have to transport the blind, and how much you are willing to spend. Portable blinds come in all shapes and sizes. The simplest blind I've used is the Apache Pyramid Blind. It resembles two sides of a pyramid, and is constructed of camo cloth on two triangular frames. It folds up to a bundle 3 feet long (1 m) and 2 inches (5 cm) around and can be slung over your shoulder as you carry it in. The Pop Up blind sets up and looks like a large umbrella with a drape around it that reaches to the ground. The Black Hole and Buddy Bucket are large cylindrical blinds that can be hung from a tree limb or a portable frame. The Double Bull and several other models are standard four wall tent types with flat or slanted roofs. The Bale Blind uses fiberglass poles and looks like a large round bale of corn or hay. All of these blinds can be used for either archery or gun hunting. The Pop Top blind was primarily designed for duck and goose hunters. It has a steel frame, a hammock seat, and a shock-corded top that flies back when you step on foot pedal. It also has a waterproof floor and can be set in 1 or 2 inches (2.5 to 5 cm) of water without getting wet inside. Although it is not really suitable for archery

hunting it makes a very comfortable gun blind. If you don't want to pack a portable blind into your area you can stuff a 4 foot by 8 foot (1.25 to 2.5 meter) piece of camouflage netting in your pocket or fanny pack, and drape it over a bush.

Archery blinds can also be used effectively in corn and sunflower fields, grassy lowlands, cattail swamps, and tall grassy areas, as in Conservation Reserve Programs (CRP). They can also be used in brushy regrowth areas in clear cuts, and at the edges of logging roads, power lines or fire lanes. My favorite regrowth spots are near thick stands of trees that the deer use as a staging area in the evening, and as a loafing area in the morning before they go back to their daytime bedding areas.

Other than being in the right place at the right time, there are three keys to using a portable blind for archery hunting. The first two keys are getting close enough for a shot and keeping the blind from spooking the deer. You have to place the blind close enough to a trail or travel corridor that the deer will pass by within your personal shooting distance, but you don't want the deer to be alarmed by the blind.

There are two ways to keep deer from spooking at a portable blind. Use a blind with a camouflage pattern that blends in with the surrounding area and use tree limbs or brush to breakup the outline of the blind. Or, set the blind up far enough in advance of when you plan to use it that the deer become accustomed to it. I usually set up my portable blinds from three to seven days before I plan to hunt from them. It doesn't take deer long to get accustomed to a new object in their area if they don't hear or smell anything that alarms them, and it doesn't move in a way that's threatening. If it's legal to feed deer during the season I also place some type of bait within 10 yards (9 m) of the stand, to get the deer to come close to the blind, while learning they have nothing to fear from it. I remove all of the bait one or two days before I plan to hunt.

The third key to using a blind for archery hunting is to make sure you have one or more shooting lanes free of obstructions. Being on the ground means there may be a lot more vegetation in the way than there is when you hunt from an elevated stand. Either put the blind where you have a clear shot or create a shooting lane. I usually cut small trees and brush off and use it to break up the outline of the blind. In corn and sunflower fields, and in tall grass and cattails or reeds, I bend the stalks over just below the window of the blind, and again use some of the stalks to break up the outline of the blind.

Permanent Blinds

Because a blind is used in a high use deer area and because one of the ways to keep deer from spooking from a blind is to leave it out long enough that the deer become accustomed to it, permanent blinds can be used in these areas. Although permanent blinds are often associated with private leases and with hunting the scrub brush areas of the southwest, they can also be used on small hunting properties in any area. Permanent blinds really come into their own in northern regions where the

Permanent deer stands, like this enclosed "shack" on stilts, can provide a hunter with both concealment and comfort.

weather can be cold, windy and wet. The addition of a small catalytic heater to add heat to a blind that keeps you out of the wind and keeps you dry allows you to hunt longer in all types of weather, especially those damp, snowy or drizzly days during the rut when bucks tend to move all day long.

Permanent blinds are usually constructed of wood or metal and covered with wood or waterproof camouflage material. They can be as simple as a wooden box with shooting ports and no amenities, large enough for only one hunter, or as complex as a multi-person hut, with sliding windows, a heater, and covered with camouflage material or painted to match the surrounding terrain and vegetation. I've even heard of hunters taking along a portable radio or television so they can keep track of their favorite football games.

I've had several hunters scoff at the idea of using permanent blinds because they don't believe deer will go anywhere near them. Then I ask them how many times they've seen deer trails going by junked farm machinery, cars, appliances and old buildings. Most of them admit that they have, more than once. The longer any product of human ingenuity has been in an area, the more accustomed to it the deer become. The rub route of one of the bucks I studied for several years passes within 5 yards (4.5 m) of an old chicken house. Knowing the buck used the route in the morning as he went back to his bedding area, I sat on an old 5-gallon (5 liter) oilcan I found in the house, and watched through one of the windows as the buck walked by within 5 yards (4.5 m).

When you see deer sign near something that can be used as a blind, take advantage of it. On one of the properties where I did deer and turkey research there were several trails and rubs within 50 yards (45 m) of an old combine, and a large chemical tank used to apply liquid fertilizer to the farm fields. On another property the deer walked within 5 yards (4.5 m) of an abandoned farmhouse, a broken down barn, and a VW bug. A hunter could easily stand in the hopper of the combine, cut a door and a shooting port in the chemical tank, or sit in the old house, barn or VW and take a deer as it walked by.

Author's Afterword

The most important thing to know when you are deer hunting, is where and when to set up. When you're hunting you need to know where the deer are likely to be during legal shooting hours. In order to know where the deer are most likely to be, you have to have an idea of when and where deer normally move during the day. Throughout the year, deer move more during the day than they do at night. However, this changes as summer turns to fall, and as the rut progresses. As the vegetation begins to die off in the fall, the food sources in wooded areas are depleted. When the leaves begin to fall from the trees, deer seek food in more open areas. They are more insecure during the day in open areas, so they become more active during the night.

Hunters rarely think about nighttime deer movement because they can't hunt at night. But an understanding of where and how deer move at night is essential if you want to be a successful hunter. During the fall of 1999, I decided not to hunt the opening of the gun season. Instead, I parked my truck on a high hill where I could watch the hunters as they drove to their hunting spots. In this way I could learn how the deer reacted to all those vehicles driving down the county roads and into the woods and fields, and all those hunters walking through the woods during the early morning hours.

I couldn't believe the number of vehicles I saw driving into and through the fields and woods where I knew the deer would be feeding at night. As I drove down the county roads to the hill, I saw five vehicles parked on access ramps to logging roads that led into wooded areas. Didn't the hunters know that the deer regularly used the logging roads and often crossed the county road right where they had parked their vehicles? Didn't

they know that any deer that saw the vehicles would probably not use the trail, and probably would not have returned to their normal bedding area because the vehicles were there?

I watched one truck go across a ½-mile-wide (0.8 km) cornfield, and then stop within 50 yards (45 m) of the woods. The hunters didn't realize that the deer were feeding in the field when they drove across it. They didn't realize that every deer in the field headed for the woods the minute they saw the headlights or heard the truck. They didn't realize every deer in the woods also heard the truck and that none of them would come out after sunrise when the saw the truck in the field.

I watched as another truck was parked on a county road within 20 yards (18 m) of a hay field where I saw deer feeding from September through January. The hunters didn't know that the deer regularly stopped there for a last-minute bite of alfalfa before they went back to their bedding areas in the morning. No wonder those hunters saw so few deer, and rarely saw a buck—let alone a big buck! They let every deer in their hunting area know it was the opening of gun season and that the woods were being invaded by humans carrying guns.

The only reason hunters cross open fields to get to their deer stands is that they don't understand that the deer eat in those fields at night. The only reason hunters park their vehicles where they do is because they don't know that deer use access ramps as crossing areas, and logging roads as travel lanes as they move to and from their wooded bedding areas at dawn and dusk. Don't cross an open field as you go to a stand in the morning! Know where the deer feeding areas, crossings, and travel routes are. Don't park where the deer can see or hear vehicles when they use those areas.

Many hunters realize that they see deer most often at dawn and dusk, but some of them fail to understand that the deer rest in wooded areas during most of the day, get up around sunset, and move out of the woods and into fields after dark. They also don't understand that when the weather is nice, the deer often spend the night eating and resting in or near fields, and that around sunrise they leave the fields to go back to their wooded bedding areas. During the night I regularly check the feeding areas where I do research and hunt. While I often see deer feeding after sunset and before sunrise, I also see them bedded in or near the fields from 10 to 12 p.m. and from 2 to 4 a.m. Several different studies on daily deer activity show that during the fall, deer are most active at night around dawn and dusk, and from 12 to 2 a.m. This means they are not moving much between 10 and 12 p.m., and between 2 and 4 a.m.

So what do deer do at night? When deer leave their bedding areas at sunset they often head for the nearest field, stopping to feed on grass, sedges, forbs, fruits and twigs along the way. Once they get to the field they stock up on corn, soybeans, alfalfa or whatever else is available. In areas where there are several types of forage, the deer may travel to each of them during the first few hours of darkness. The deer don't actually digest what they eat while feeding because they are ruminants. They store the food until later. Once they are full the deer usually lay down to regurgitate their cud and chew it to make it digestible. From the daily activity studies I mentioned earlier it appears that deer feed for a couple hours in the evening, lay down to rest and chew their cud for a couple of hours, then get up and feed for another couple of hours after midnight. They rest again for a couple of hours, and then get up to feed again for a couple hours before going back to their bedding areas. It is thought that deer rarely sleep longer than two hours before standing up to at least stretch. During the winter deer may sleep longer than that. During the rut bucks may bed very little.

While I was watching the hunters during the first day of the gun season one year, I noticed three does, each with a fawn, feeding in the cornfields within half a mile of my truck. Because these deer were not harassed by hunters they continued to feed until about 8:30 a.m. Even with several gunshots around them they continued to feed, and appeared not to be alarmed by the gunshots in the woods. Shortly after 8:30, the does and fawns moved north and crossed a county road in open country. Then they went north until they got close to a group of trees planted along a neighbor's driveway as a windbreak/snow fence. They followed the trees east and crossed a highway, and eventually moved back into the wooded area where they bedded.

I suspect the deer were unaware of the hunters stationed in those woods and therefore, they continued to move and feed as they normally would. They probably didn't stop moving and feeding until they got back to their bedding areas, which may have taken an hour or more. Movement by deer such as these, unaware of hunters, explains why hunters often see deer moving in wooded areas late in the morning even during the hunting season. Hunters who know that this activity may occur can take advantage of it by staying in the woods most of the day. They may even see a buck following a doe late in the morning during the rut, especially if the does have been feeding in fields away from their bedding areas.

Appendix

Whitetail Subspecies

The whitetails of North America range in size as follows: The largest are the northern woodland, Dakota and northwest subspecies.

The smallest are the Florida Key deer, the Carmen Mountains/Fantail deer and the Coues deer.

The Columbian whitetail subspecies and the Key deer were both on the Endangered Species List in 1989.

US Distribution

- Northern woodland whitetail *(O. v. borealis)* – eastern shore of North America to the Mississippi River and the eastern half of Minnesota, from south of Hudson Bay to northern Virginia and northern Tennessee.

- Dakota whitetail *(O. v. dakotensis)* – western Minnesota, southern Manitoba, Saskatchewan and Alberta to the Continental Divide, down to northern Colorado.

- Northwest whitetail *(O. v. ochrorous)* – southern British Columbia, western Montana, Idaho and areas of Washington and Oregon east of the Cascade Mountains.

- Columbian whitetail *(O. v. leucurus)* – west of the Cascade Mountains in Washington and northern Oregon.

- Virginia whitetail *(O. v. virginianus)* – northern Virginia south of the Ohio River west to the Mississippi River, and south to Mississippi and the northern portion of the Florida Panhandle.

- Florida coastal whitetail *(O. v. osceola)* – south of this range to the Gulf Of Mexico to eastern Florida.

- Florida whitetail *(O. v. seminolus)* – eastern portions of Florida.

- Florida Key *(O. v. clavium)* – keys off the western coast of Florida.

- Kansas whitetail *(O. v. macrorus)* – west of the Mississippi from south of the Minnesota River to the Missouri River along the Missouri/Arkansas/Louisiana state lines, to southern Louisiana.

- Avery Island whitetail *(O. v. mcilhennyi)* – coastal areas of Louisiana and Texas to Galveston Bay.

- Texas whitetail *(O. v. texanus)* – northern Mexico, Texas, Oklahoma, Kansas and Nebraska, north to the Niobrara River in Nebraska and west to the Rocky Mountain foothills.

- Carmen Mountains *(O. v. carminis)* – Big Bend National Forest in Texas and north central Mexico.

- Coues, pronounced "cows," whitetail *(O. v. couesi)* – southern New Mexico and Arizona, west of the Continental Divide to the Gulf of California east of the Rio Grande River.

- Bull's Island whitetail *(O. v. taurinsulae)*, the Hunting Island whitetail *(O. v. venatorius)*, the Hilton Head Island whitetail *(O. v. hiltonensis)* and the Blackbeard Island whitetails *(O. v. nigribarbis)* – Islands of those names off the Georgia coast.

Central America and South America Distribution

- Acapulco whitetail *(O. v. acapulcensis)* – southern Mexico

- Chiapas whitetail *(O. v. oaxacensis)* – southern Mexico

- Chiriqui whitetail *(O. v. chiriquensis)* – Panama.

- Mexican lowland whitetail *(O. v. thomasi)* – southeastern Mexico, Mexican whitetail *(O. v. mexicanus)* – central Mexico.

- Miquihuan whitetail *(O. v. miquihuanensis)* – central Mexico.

- Nicaragua whitetail *(O. v. truei)* – Nicaragua and adjacent states.

- Nelson's whitetail *(O. v. nelsoni)* – southern Mexico and Guatamala.

- Northern Veracruz whitetail *(O. v. veraecrucis)* – eastern Mexico.

- Perunvian whitetail *(O. v. peruvianus)* – Peru.

- Rain forest whitetail *(O.v. toltecus)* – southern Mexico.

- Rothchild's whitetail *(O. v. rothschildi)* – Coiba Island, Panama.

- Sinaloa whitetail *(O. v. sinaloae)* – mid western Mexico.

- Venado whitetail *(O. v. goudotii)* – Columbia *(Andes)* and West Venzuela.

- Venado whitetail *(O. v. curassavicus)* – Curacao Island.

- Venado whitetail *(O. v. eustus)* – Ecuador.

- Venado whitetail *(O. v. cariacou)* – French Guiana and North Brazil.

- Venado whitetail *(O. v. margaritae)* – Margarita Islands.

- Venado whitetail *(O. v. gymnotis)* – Venzuela and Guianas.

- Venado whitetail *(O. v. tropicalis)* – western Columbia.

- Yucatan whitetail *(O. v. yucatanensis)* – Yucatan and Honduras.

Glossary of Terms

Bed: The place where a deer has lain down, evident by pressed-down grass, leaves or dirt creating a rough oval or kidney shape.

Bedding Site: The actual site where a deer lays down. Deer generally use different bedding sites during the day and night. See Daytime an Nighttime Bedding Sites.

Breeding Period: The time frame from when the first does are bred until the last does are bred. In the northern states breeding often occurs from mid October to late December, about 75 days. In southern states breeding may occur as early as mid September and last until late February, but generally from mid October to mid January, 90 days or more.

Buck Trail: A lightly traveled trail used by bucks, often paralleling the more heavily used doe trails, but farther into cover, or up or down the hill, sometimes evident by rubs on small trees near the trail, and by relatively few, but large, tracks.

Core Area: The area where a deer spends the majority of its time during the day, and where it usually lies down to rest during the day. Because deer are security conscious they often spend the day where they can't see, hear or smell predators, especially humans and human-related activity. The core area is often in thick brush or woods, and may contain some open areas where the deer can eat during the day without exposing itself. Core areas may range in size from as little as 2 to 3 acres (0.8 to 1.2 ha) to more than 180 acres (72 ha), depending on the habitat. The larger the brushy or wooded area is, the larger the core area can be.

Daytime Bedding Sites: The sites within the core area where the deer lie down during the day.

Dispersal Phase: I also refer to this as the Transition Phase. The time frame in late summer/early fall when buck groups begin to break up, when all deer begin to switch from summer home ranges to fall home ranges, and when bucks begin to expand their home ranges in preparation for the rut. This may start as early as the last week of August/first week of September in the north and continue into October. This phase is in progress when deer are no longer seen in summer feeding areas, when bucks are no longer seen traveling together, when rubs and scrapes appear in new/previously unused locations.

Doe Trail: Deer trails that are heavily used, primarily by does and fawns (they may be used by bucks during the rut). They are usually evident by the lack of vegetation on the ground in the fall, and by the numbers of different sized tracks on the trail.

Early Breeding Phase: I also refer to this as the Peak Scraping Phase. This is when some does come into estrus before the Primary Breeding Phase. It may occur from late September to mid October in the northern states and Canada. Approximately the same time frame as the Scraping Phase. See Scraping Phase.

Home Range: This generally refers to the area used by a deer throughout the year. It may also be referred to as an annual home range. Depending on the climate and the habitat, deer may also have one or more seasonal home ranges that they use in the spring, summer, fall and winter.

Horning: The performance of a buck as it rubs its forehead, sides of the head, and antlers on a licking branch or an overhanging branch at a scrape. Also called Thrashing.

Late Breeding Phase: This is when some six-month-old doe fawns, and unhealthy or older does, may come into a first estrus, and when does that did not get bred during the primary breeding phase may come into another estrus. Both dominant and subdominant bucks move in travel corridors and along rub routes and scrape lines in search of estrus does at this time. This phase may last for two or more weeks, but it is usually not as intense as the primary breeding phase. Because the bucks are interested in breeding, they move in travel corridors, and along rub routes and scrape lines leading to doe core areas and food sources and they frequent doe core areas and food sources looking for receptive does.

Licking Branch: A low-hanging branch, usually 3 to 4 feet (1 to 1¼ m) above the ground, often with the tips of the branch and leaves mutilated or chewed off. Both bucks and does may lick, chew and rub the branch with their foreheads in order to leave scent on the branch. This scent may express the sex, age and dominance status of the deer that left it. Although there may be a scrape under the licking branch, there need not be scrape for the branch to be used as a licking branch by the deer. Licking branches may be used by both sexes and all ages of deer throughout the year. The ground under the licking branch may be pawed and turned into a scrape during the rut. When a licking branch does occur over a scrape the branch is referred to as an overhanging branch. See Overhanging Branch.

Nighttime Bedding Sites: The areas where deer bed at night, often in or near food sources. Although deer generally sleep during the day and feed at night, they often bed down to rest, ruminate, and sleep near nighttime food sources. The vision of many predators is limited at night, but because deer can see well enough to detect danger, they feel more secure in open areas at night than they do during the day. Therefore, they may bed in open areas, often out of the wind, during the night. Night beds can often be found in fields, at field edges, and in nearby brushy and grassy areas.

Overhanging Branch: Also called a Licking Branch. A low-hanging branch over a scrape, usually 3 to 4 feet (1 to 1¼ m) off the ground, that may be used by all ages and both sexes of deer, but, particularly used by bucks during the rut. The deer may lick, chew and rub the branch with their forehead in order to leave scent, which may express the sex, age and dominance status of the deer that left it. See Licking Branch.

Patterning: The term used to describe when a hunter walks a rub route to locate a buck's core area, and watches the rub route to determine when the buck uses specific portions of its route during the day, in order to determine the best locations and times to hunt the buck.

Pawing: When a buck uses its front hooves to remove vegetation, leaves, debris or dirt from the ground while creating a scrape. See Scraping.

Peak of the Rut, Peak Rut: The one week during the primary breeding phase when most of the does are bred. In the northern United States and Canada this usually occurs during the first to second week of November. It is almost impossible to predict a day or a week when this will happen, because not all does are bred at the same time. Because so few does get bred during any one day, all it takes to change the timing of the peak of the rut is for one more doe to be bred during one week than on any other week.

Peak Scraping: The time frame when most scraping occurs. Peak scraping often begins two to three weeks before peak breeding, and usually lasts until several does come into estrus at the same time. Peak scraping may last up to three weeks, from about mid October to early November in the northern states and Canada. This is when bucks begin to travel rub routes making rubs and scrapes. Scrapes opening up/being used semi-regularly in wooded/secure areas are a sign that the bucks may be traveling their rub routes during the day, and a sign that scrape activity is beginning to peak. Some does may come into estrus at this time. This is the phase of the rut when bucks are most predictable in their daily movements. See Scraping Phase.

Pheromones: A substance secreted by an animal and released for detection and response by another animal of the same species. Whitetails produce scents from the tarsal glands on the inside of the rear legs, the metatarsal glands on the outside of the rear legs, the interdigital glands between the hooves of each foot, and the forehead glands on the top of the head. They may possibly produce scents from the nasal glands inside the nose, the preorbital glands at the front of the eye, the penal glands inside the penal sheath, and the salivary glands inside the mouth.

Post-Primary Breeding Phase: This phase starts shortly after the primary breeding phase ends, after the majority of the does have been bred. It may last up to three weeks, depending on the buck-to-doe ratio of the deer herd in the area, and the number of six-month-old doe fawns and one-year-old does. It often occurs during the last part of November and first weeks of December in the northern states. Does may still

be coming into estrus at this time. Subdominant bucks may come into rut condition at this time and begin to scrape and look for does. Dominant bucks may begin scraping again, and may continue to look for does. Because some does are still in estrus, and the bucks are in rut, scraping, trolling and chasing activity may occur throughout the day, especially at dawn and dusk in travel corridors, along rub routes and near scrape lines leading to doe core areas and food sources.

Post-Rut: This follows the late breeding phase, after most of the does have been bred. In northern states it often occurs about two months after peak breeding, usually in late December/early January. This is when bucks may begin to travel, sometimes together, to food sources to gain back the weight they lost during the early, primary and late breeding phases. At this time, the does' primary interests are in putting on weight to get them through the winter and to provide nutritional requirements during pregnancy. Most buck activity will be from early afternoon to evening as they move along travel corridors leading to food sources, and in the morning along travel corridors as they move back to their core areas and bedding sites.

Pre-Late Breeding Phase: This rut phase may begin from one to three weeks after the end of peak breeding. It usually occurs from late November to early December in the northern states. This is when both dominant and subdominant bucks may leave their core areas and begin to move in travel corridors, and along rub routes and scrape lines in search of estrus does after the rest phase. Many does may be between estrus cycles, but some may come into estrus at this time. Most buck activity will be at dawn and dusk in travel corridors along rub routes and scrape lines leading to doe core areas and food sources.

Pre-Primary Breeding Phase: Also called the Early Breeding Phase and the Scraping Phase. The two- to three-week time frame preceding the primary breeding phase. Approximately the same time frame as peak scraping, usually the last two weeks of October and first week of November in the northern states. Some does may come into estrus, and be bred, at this time. See Peak Scraping.

Pre-Rut Phase: Approximately the same time frame as the rubbing phase, from the time when bucks begin to shed velvet in late August/early September to mid October in the northern states. This is when bucks begin rubbing to remove velvet, usually in their core areas, often near bedding sites. Rubbing may occur as much as three months before peak breeding. Dominant bucks may begin to scrape shortly after shedding velvet, primarily at licking branches near field edges/food sources at dawn and dusk, and in secure areas during the day. Does do not normally come into estrus during this phase.

Primary Breeding Phase: This is when the majority of the does come into estrus. This phase may last two weeks or more, from the first to the third weeks of November in the northern states and Canada. Does coming into estrus cause dominant bucks to scrape less and travel more in their search for receptive partners. Subdominant bucks may begin to scrape during this phase because the dominants are busy trolling for, chasing, and breeding does. Deer movement may occur anytime and anywhere.

Rest Phase: This rut phase occurs after most of the does have been bred during the primary breeding phase, when bucks return to their core areas to rest and eat to gain back the fat they lost during the breeding phase so they can make it through the rest of the winter. This phase generally begins two to three weeks after peak breeding, usually in mid to late November in northern states. Most of the does are between estrus cycles at this time. Although does may move to normal food sources, bucks may stay in or near their core areas, seldom showing themselves during daylight hours.

Rub: The portion of a tree that has been rubbed by a buck with its antlers, usually with the bark rubbed off, exposing the light-colored wood beneath, creating a visual clue that the tree has been rubbed by a buck. The buck leaves scent from its forehead glands on the tree as it rubs. This scent tells other deer the age and social status of the buck creating the rub.

Rubbing: The performance of a buck as it rubs a tree or bush with its antlers and forehead leaving forehead scent on the tree. Brush and small trees may be mangled and broken in this process.

Rubbing Phase: Also called the Pre-Rut. This phase begins when bucks rub their antlers on bushes and small trees to remove the dried velvet from the antlers. Rubbing may begin as early as late August and last until early January in the northern states and Canada, and longer in the south. It often continues as long as there are does are in estrus. Peak rubbing usually occurs prior to peak scraping, often in late September or early October. Bucks may begin rubbing on larger trees as the rut progresses for several reasons: as an act of redirected aggression; to leave scent on the tree as a sign of dominance and breeding readiness to all other deer in the area; in order to build up their neck muscles in anticipation of sparring matches and fights with other bucks. See Pre-Rut.

Rub Route: The trail a buck uses, sometimes evident by rubbed trees on or near the trail. The rubbed trees may be as close together as 5 feet (1.5 m), or as far apart as ½ mile (0.8 km) or more along the rub route. The side of the tree on which the rubs appear indicate the direction of the buck's travel along the route. Rub routes usually lead from the buck's core area/daytime bedding site to a food source used by bucks and does at night during the fall rut. If there are trees along the entire rub route the route may eventually lead back to the buck's core areas. A rub route may be used by more than one buck, and may be traveled in both directions. A buck may have more than one rub route.

Rub-Urinate: The action of a deer when it hunches its back and places its back legs under its body so that it can urinate over the tarsal glands on the inside of its rear legs. The

resultant smell, a combination of urine and the pheromone from the tarsal gland, is used as a recognition scent by whitetails. Deer can tell the age and sex of other deer by the scents from the tarsal gland. All deer rub-urinate throughout the year, often upon rising from their beds. Bucks rub-urinate more frequently during the rut, especially at scrapes, to let both bucks and does know their social status, and to let does know their health and breeding readiness.

Scents: Products used to attract deer while hunting. Scents fall into four basic categories: deer-based attractants, food and other attractants, cover scents, and blocking scents. Deer based attractants include buck and doe urine, buck-in-rut urine and estrus doe urine (both supposedly collected during the rut), and substances from the forehead gland, tarsal gland and interdigital gland. These substances may be used individually, in combination with each other, or with food and other attractants. Food and other attractants include products that smell like corn, acorns, vanilla, anise, licorice, molasses, dirt or "secret" man-made formulas. Cover scents, used to overpower or disguise the smells associated with humans include scents or urine from coyotes, fox, raccoon and cow, and the smell of vegetation such as pine needles and sap, maple and oak leaves, and sage. Blocking scents, are used to keep a deer from using routes where the hunter is not located, in order to redirect deer to a route the where the hunter is located, includes alarm scents from deer, and scents from dogs, wolves and humans. See Pheromones.

Scrape: The ground underneath an overhanging branch that has been pawed by a buck. After several uses, all vegetation may be removed from the ground, exposing the soil. A scrape is often evident by a pile of vegetation, leaves, dirt or other debris at the back of the scrape. Scrapes used at night are often found at field and meadow edges, and in open areas. Scrapes used during the day are often found in wooded or secluded areas.

Scrape Line: A series of scrapes in a rough line or clustered together, often along a trail or rub route used by the buck during the rut. Scrape lines or clusters of scrapes are often found in travel corridors, creek bottoms, benches on the sides of hills, along unused or overgrown roads in wooded areas, in semi-open areas near food sources, and in field edges.

Scraping: The action of a buck as it approaches an overhanging branch, licks, chews, horns or thrashes the branch, paws the ground under the branch, and then rub-urinates in or near the pawed area. Specifically, the performance of a buck when it scrapes away vegetation, leaves, dirt and other debris and creates an area of bare ground (a scrape) under a licking branch or an overhanging branch. The buck may paw the ground from one to five times with first one hoof and then the other, leaving gouges in the ground from the points of its hooves. Vegetation, leaves and dirt may be pushed toward the rear of the scrape as the buck paws the ground, creating a small pile. Prior to scraping bucks usually lick and chew the overhanging branch, rub it with their forehead, and horn it with their antlers. Scraping results in a complex set of scents and visual signs that expresses dominance and breeding readiness to all other deer in the area. The scents at the scrape may stimulate does to come into estrus, and help synchronize the timing of the rut between the bucks and does.

Scraping Phase: Also called the Pre-Primary Breeding or Early Breeding Phase. The time frame when most scraping occurs during the rut. Scraping usually begins as soon as the bucks shed the velvet from their antlers. This may start as early as late August and last until early January in the northern states and Canada. It may begin earlier and last longer in southern states. Scraping may begin to significantly increase during the last two weeks of October in the northern states and Canada, with actual peak scraping occurring from the last two weeks of October to the first or second week of November.

Shed: A shed is an antler that has fallen from a buck's head, usually in early winter. Depending on their age and health, bucks may begin to shed their antlers as early as December and as late as March. As long as does are in estrus a buck's testosterone level may remain elevated, and as long as the testosterone level is elevated the buck may retain its antlers.

Shedding Velvet: The loss of the soft hairy skin that covers the buck's antlers as they grow. Shedding velvet is triggered by shorter daylight hours in the fall and a rise in testosterone level of the buck.

Staging Area: Semi-open, sometimes secluded areas where deer stop and may congregate before entering open feeding areas in the late afternoon or early evening.

The Rut: The time frame when bucks and does come into breeding condition; it applies to all phases of the rut. The preparation for breeding begins when bucks shed velvet, as early as late August in the north. The rut usually ends after the late breeding phase, after the majority of the does have been bred, which may be as early as late December in the north, and as late as March in the south. In areas where there are low buck-to-doe ratios, and where not all of the does are bred during their first or second estrus, the does may experience a third or even a fourth estrus and be bred at that time, which creates a longer than normal rut.

Thrashing: Also called horning. The term used to describe the action of a buck when it aggressively rubs or fights brush or small trees with its antlers, often leaving the brush or tree mangled or broken. This may occur when a buck is in the presence of another buck as a dominance display of redirected aggression. Sites where several trees have been thrashed and brush is mangled may indicate areas used by two or more bucks of equal social status, often dominants. See Horning.

Transition Zone: Areas traveled by deer that are between wooded areas and open feeding areas, swamps, brushy areas and semi-open woods. See Travel Corridor.

Travel Corridor: Travel corridors are areas where one or more deer trails lead to and from core areas and food sources. They occur in wooded fingers, strips of woods, wooded streambeds and river bottoms, benches on hillsides in wooded areas, brushy areas between wooded areas/food sources, and other areas that restrict deer movement because of terrain or vegetation.

Velvet: The soft hairy skin covering a buck's antlers as they grow.

Walk the Rub Route, Walking a Rub Route: This is the term used when a hunter follows a buck trail with visual rubs along it, the purpose being to locate the areas frequented by the buck, particularly its daytime core area. A rub route is usually followed backward, in the direction from which the buck came, with the visible portion of the rub behind the hunter as they walk.

Deer Camp Supply List

- Sleeping bag (3# plus synthetic), sleeping pad and ground sheet or small folding cot if sleeping on the ground
- Large duffel bag
- Rain gear or poncho
- Orange vest and hat (gun hunters)
- Camera, film, extra batteries
- Two flashlights, extra batteries

- Weather band radio, extra batteries
- Knives (skinner and pocket), bone saw, knife sharpener
- Gun or bow, hard-sided case, extra ammunition
- License, tags and hunter safety card if needed
- Pack frame

- Game bags
- 48-quart (48 liter) cooler
- First-aid kit
- Binoculars and/or spotting scope
- Multi-tool

Personal Gear List

- Lightweight socks, underwear, handkerchiefs
- Light and medium polypropylene underwear and socks
- Wool/insulated waterproof boot liners
- Camp shoes, lightweight knee-high rubber boots, insulated pac boots with extra liners
- Heavy and light jackets, pants, hats and gloves in camouflage fleece or wool
- Lightweight hat, insulated waterproof hat
- Towels, toiletries

- Medications
- 20-pound (9 kg) Day Pack to be worn daily for survival
- Army-style poncho (with grommets and snaps to use as rain gear, or to make a lean-to)
- 20 feet of ¼-inch (6 m of 62 mm) rope or parachute cord
- Two compasses, topographical map, flagging, GPS device
- Flares, signaling whistle and mirror, two-way radio and/or cell phone
- First-aid kit and daily medication

- Four lighters, three fire starters (Sterno, candles etc. in case wood is wet)
- Space/emergency blanket
- Extra socks and underwear
- Heavy polypropylene underwear
- Sweater and heavy stocking cap
- Instant soup, instant chocolate, granola bars, candy bars, dried fruit
- Cup (to heat water), 2-quart (2 liter) canteen of water
- Water purification tablets
- Large knife or hatchet and multi-tool

Resources

ATSKO / Sno Seal
www.atsko.com

Cabela's
www.cabelas.com

Contain Clothing
www.TRMichels.com

Darton Archery
www.dartonarchery.com

Delta Decoys
www.deltatargets.com

Double Bull Archery
www.doublebull.com

Eliminator Clothing
www.TRMichels.com

Federal Cartridge Corporation
www.federalcartridge.com

Field Stalker Camouflage
www.TRMichels.com

Kolpin
www.kolpin.com

Konifer Camouflage
www.TRMichels.com

La Crosse Footwear
www.lacrosse.com

O. F. Mossberg & Sons
www.mossberg.com

Outdoor Edge Cutlery Corp.
www.outdooredge.com

Robinson Outdoors, Inc.
www.robinsonlabs.com

Silver Creek Industries
www.silvercreek.com

Total Camouflage
www.TRMichels.com

Trail Timer Game Monitors
www.trailtimer.com

Walls Industries, Inc.
www.wallsoutdoors.com

Wildlife Research Center
www.wildlife.com

Index

Photo Credits

Greg "Dr. Juice" Bambenek
© Dr. Juice: pp. 8, 70, 78, 88, 91, 98, 101, 113, back cover (top & bottom)

Tim Christie
Coeur D'Alene, Idaho
© Tim Christie/TimChristiePhoto.com: front cover deer

Creative Publishing International
© Creative Publishing International: pp. 126

Mark Emery
Ocala, Florida
© Mark Emery: pp. 30 (left), 30 (right), 33, 44, 51, 100, 105

Brooks Johnson
© Double Bull Archery: pp. 93, 118, 128, 130

Gary Kramer
Willows, California
© garykramer.net: pp. 46

John D. LaMere
Apple Valley, Minnesota
© John D. LaMere: pp. 31, 32, 124

Tawnya & T.R. Michels
Burnsville, Minnesota
© T. R. Michels Photography
www.TRMichels.com

Mark Raycroft
Trenton, Ontario, Canada
© Mark Raycroft: pp. 6, 13, 21, 38, 55, 56, 66, 84, 85, 106, 117

Ken Thommes
Hillman, Minnesota
© Ken Thommes: pp. 94, 96, 109

US National Park Service
© pp. 34

US Department of Agriculture © pp. 11

Wildlife Research Center
© pp. 60, 102, 110, 112, 133, back cover (middle)

Wisconsin Department of Natural Resources
© pp. 19, 26, 28, 65, 82, 133

Creative Publishing international
Your Complete Source of How-to Information for the Outdoors

Hunting Books
- Advanced Turkey Hunting
- Advanced Whitetail Hunting
- Black Bear Hunting
- Bowhunting Equipment & Skills
- Bowhunter's Guide to Accurate Shooting
- The Complete Guide to Hunting
- Dog Training
- Elk Hunting
- How to Think Like a Survivor
- Hunting Record-Book Bucks
- Mule Deer Hunting
- Muzzleloading
- Outdoor Guide to Using Your GPS
- Pronghorn Hunting
- Waterfowl Hunting
- Whitetail Hunting
- Whitetail Techniques & Tactics
- Wild Turkey

Fishing Books
- Advanced Bass Fishing
- The Art of Freshwater Fishing
- The Complete Guide to Freshwater Fishing

- Fishing for Catfish
- Fishing Rivers & Streams
- Fishing Tips & Tricks
- Fishing with Artificial Lures
- Inshore Salt Water Fishing
- Kids Gone Campin'
- Kids Gone Fishin'
- Largemouth Bass
- Live Bait Fishing
- Modern Methods of Ice Fishing
- Northern Pike & Muskie
- Offshore Salt Water Fishing
- Panfish
- Salt Water Fishing Tactics
- Smallmouth Bass
- Striped Bass Fishing: Salt Water Strategies
- Successful Walleye Fishing
- Trout
- Ultralight Fishing

Fly Fishing Books
- The Art of Fly Tying
- The Art of Fly Tying – CD-ROM
- Complete Photo Guide to Fly Fishing

- Complete Photo Guide to Fly Tying
- Fishing Dry Flies
- Fishing Nymphs, Wet Flies & Streamers
- Fly-Fishing Equipment & Skills
- Fly Fishing for Beginners
- Fly Fishing for Trout in Streams
- Fly-Tying Techniques & Patterns

Cookbooks
- All-Time Favorite Game Bird Recipes
- America's Favorite Fish Recipes
- America's Favorite Wild Game Recipes
- Backyard Grilling
- Cooking Wild in Kate's Camp
- Cooking Wild in Kate's Kitchen
- Dressing & Cooking Wild Game
- The New Cleaning & Cooking Fish
- Preparing Fish & Wild Game
- The Saltwater Cookbook
- Venison Cookery
- The Wild Butcher

To purchase these or other Creative Publishing international titles,
contact your local bookseller, or visit our website at
www.creativepub.com

The Complete
FLY FISHERMAN™